BODIES IN PIECES

*Fantastic Narrative and the
Poetics of the Fragment*

Bodies in Pieces

FANTASTIC NARRATIVE AND THE
POETICS OF THE FRAGMENT

DEBORAH A. HARTER

STANFORD UNIVERSITY PRESS

Stanford, California   1996

Stanford University Press
Stanford, California
© 1996 by the Board of Trustees of the
Leland Stanford Junior University

Printed in the United States of America

CIP data appear at the end of the book

Stanford University Press publications
are distributed exclusively by Stanford
University Press within the United States,
Canada, Mexico, and Central America;
they are distributed exclusively by
Cambridge University Press
throughout the rest of the world.

Publication of this work was
underwritten in part by a
grant from Rice University.

For my mother and father,
and for Tim and Sydney

Acknowledgments

To the many who supported me during the writing of this book or contributed to my thinking, I owe a debt of gratitude. I wish to thank, first and foremost, Marie-Hélène Huet and D. A. Miller, whose faith in this project from its earliest phases inspired and often surpassed my own. I am deeply grateful to Leo Bersani, Robert Alter, and Hinrich Seeba, for their invaluable commentary and unfailing encouragement. For their spirited questions during that crucial period when I was only beginning to formulate my ideas, I thank Jean Andrews, Kenneth Berri, Eric Downing, Gail Finney, Tobin Siebers, and Victor Udwin; they were indispensable sounding boards. In this project's final stages I profited from the many fine suggestions of Charles Bernheimer, Lauren Berlant, Scott Derrick, Lilian Furst, Colleen Lamos, Helena Michie, Laurence Porter, and William Sharpe, each of whom read the entire manuscript or substantial portions of it. To Caroline Newman I owe a special debt. Her intelligence, her friendship, and her unsparing criticism made a difference at every point.

During the course of this project several timely fellowships made it possible to work without interruption. I would like to thank the American Council of Learned Societies (ACLS), the

American Association of University Women (AAUW), and the Chancellors of the University of California. I am grateful as well for the generous support I received from Rice University and its Dean of Humanities, Allen J. Matusow. I thank the editor and publishers of *L'Esprit créateur*, with whose permission I include here, as Chapters 1 and 2, a revised version of what appeared originally in their special issue on "Theories of the Fantastic" (vol. 28, 1989). For their marvelous copyediting I am grateful to Ann Klefstad at Stanford University Press and Terry Grasso Munisteri at Rice University. Several wonderful assistants helped me, at various stages, to get these pages to press: Yvonne Bruce, Evelyne Datta, Clara Jaeckel, and Susannah Mintz.

I would finally add, yet it is far too little, that this book would not have been written but for the moral and the poetic treasures I cherish from my mother and from the memory of my father, nor could it have been completed without the unflagging support of my husband, Tim Cochran, and my daughter Sydney. When my own body, falling to pieces, found itself in perverse symphony with my subject, their love remained ever whole.

D. A. H.

Contents

BODIES IN PIECES

*Fantastic Narrative and the
Poetics of the Fragment*

Introduction

> The body is that . . . which cries out mutely before the self-assurance of reason and propriety; it is that tapestry in which our form shifts and changes . . . ; it is the "continuous" from which we fashion, for ourselves and for others, a visible discontinuity that demands its due.
>
> —Philippe Sollers, "Le Toit: essai de lecture systématique"

Fantastic narrative of the nineteenth century is often viewed in terms of its unanchored psyches, its flights of romantic fantasy, its rendering of otherworldly states of being. Critics have underscored its link to "morbid states of the conscious mind, which . . . projects before itself images of its own anguish and terror."[1] They have pointed to the "rupture" its texts effect in the very "constants of the perceptual . . . , the moral . . . [and] the aesthetic."[2] Already in 1761 Denis Diderot and Jean Le Rond d'Alembert had, in their *Encyclopédie*, defined the larger realm from which this literary form would develop as a kind of delirium, a "disordering of the imagination," a recounting of things "most bizarre."[3] And yet fantastic narrative in the nineteenth century, the period in which it flourished, is perhaps most interesting for its fundamental preoccupation with a profoundly material, physically sensible world. Its texts often find their focus in furniture and draperies, in knickknacks and daily routine. Its concern is to read the world quite plainly, a concern that ultimately betrays this form's surprising affinities with its contemporary, the realist novel. In both realist and fantastic narrative there is a desire to articulate the visible contours of the nineteenth-century world they engage, to come to terms with and to describe a physical and historical environment of proliferating objects and deteriorating meaning.

There is a difference between these narrative forms. But this difference, I would suggest, lies far less in the world that each of these forms portrays than in the opposing ways in which they strive to recompose that world in their fiction. The realist novel points at every moment toward the wholeness of the world it represents. For all its catalogues, for all its sprawling appearance, in the end it demands, as Leo Bersani has noted, a kind of "compulsive intelligibility," a "totality of sense" (*Baudelaire and Freud*, 119–20). The novel invites us to believe in "the temporal myths of real beginnings and definitive endings" (119–20). It strives to triumph over the disarray of nineteenth-century society "by imposing upon it [its] own determined order."[4] It may be true, as D. A. Miller has shown, that the novel "continually *promises* [a] totality it cannot, at any single moment, deliver" (*Narrative and Its Discontents*, 279). Still, its overarching desire is to circumscribe and control the chaos of the contemporary world, and in this effort—in this panic—it is a continual gesture toward structured and structuring coherence.

Fantastic narrative, on the other hand, evokes this world in all its partialness. It lingers with and promotes the fragment rather than seeking the whole; it puts forth partially named or unnamed characters rather than characters with full names; it is best realized in the form of the short tale rather than in the form of the novel.[5] The loose ends and divergent energies forcibly integrated into the fabric of the realist novel are here left purposefully uncontained. Consciousness often drifts among several fragmented psyches. Endings seem inevitably to leave us hesitating. The dream of material completeness that often defies yet fundamentally defines the realist enterprise is countered here by a seeming delight in reproducing reality in its "pieces," where even the human body succumbs to morselization. In story after story, and with a kind of synechdochic fury, the body is captured and contemplated through its severed hands, its beating heart, its lost meshes of hair. Protagonists find their attention focused on such fragments as the bloody eyes of Olimpia in E. T. A. Hoffmann's "Der Sandmann" (1816), left behind when her robot body is torn apart; the skeletal hand in Guy de Maupassant's "La Main" (1883), seen one night as it "gallops" across the room moving its fingers "as though they were feet"; the "vulture eye" and hellish beating heart of a mild old man in Edgar Allan Poe's "The Tell-Tale Heart" (1843). They are dazzled by such parts of bodies as the tiny hand on Georgiana's face in Nathaniel Hawthorne's "The Birthmark" (1834); the perfect breast, in Théophile Gautier's "Arria Marcella, souvenir de Pompéi" (1852), whose ashen imprint is still perceptible in the lava of Pompeii; the angelic hand that beckons and stretches out in all its loveliness in Charles Nodier's "Une heure ou la vision" (1801).

It is this strange insistence of the fragmented body in fantastic narrative that provides the focus for the chapters to follow. How do this body's pieces function to determine fantastic discourse? From what textual and subjective violence are they produced? To whom do they belong? Why is it so often the female body that is torn apart, whether in the realm of language, within the tangible world evoked by the text, or in the arena of the narrator's partializing gaze? (Is this a sign of a violently phallocentric discourse? Is the female body more easily fetishized? Is it a question of erotics? Are the fragments of the female body the displaced markers of these tales' narrators' *own* shattered bodies?) Does the fragmented body in these texts represent a fascination in this narrative form with *all* that is fragmentary and incomplete, in contradistinction to the structured and structuring unities of the realist novel?

But this study finds, in fantastic narrative and its "discourse of the body," more than just an underlying poetics of the fragment. It finds as well that just as the novel is fraught with parts that eventually give the lie to its desperate efforts at achieving unity—constructs the human body itself in ways that ultimately reveal its careful patchwork—so the fragment in fantastic narrative betrays a certain anguished gesture toward this literary form's own, different vision of wholeness. The differing strategies of these two genres—the one pressing toward, the other away from totalization—appear a paired set of terms in a single imaginative system in which fantastic narrative becomes for the realist novel far less an opposing than a reflective other, and in which realist discourse is discovered in all its fragmented, "fantastic" nature.

*

In the course of this work I have not made it a primary goal to redefine fantastic narrative as a genre, wishing to get beyond, or at least to navigate around, the constrictions that notions of genre often produce. What I am able to say about fantastic narrative, through its often stunning mobilization of the body, does not derive from a careful scrutiny of earlier definitions of this literary form, but from a recasting of its texts in the light of a poetics of fragmentation and disfigurement. In the process I have often found it necessary to invoke those very categories and oppositions that have traditionally guided and at times misled our thinking—oppositions, for example, between the whole and the fragment, or between realism and the fantastic. But I hope my analysis will ultimately serve both to question and to enrich their usefulness. Fantastic narrative is a significant category whose history I will briefly sketch, yet its texts defy at every point any too-restrictive frame, undermine the very terms necessary to describe them.

Before Tzvetan Todorov's seminal study *Introduction à la littérature fantastique* (1970), the fantastic in literature was seen as a subversion of the natural, a threat to the rational, an escape from the "real" in the physical, social, and psychological domains. In such canonical examples of fantastic narrative as Hoffmann's "Der Sandmann," Poe's "The Black Cat," Prosper Mérimée's "La Vénus d'Ille," and Maupassant's "Le Horla," critics saw a "brutal intrusion of mystery into the everyday" (Pierre-Georges Castex), a "diametric reversal of the ground rules of a narrative world" (Eric Rabkin), the possibility of "transcending the human" (Jean-Paul Sartre).[6] In a similar spirit of escape and subversion Todorov saw fantastic narrative as a way of "speaking" otherwise unacceptable social and sexual taboos in the guise of otherworldly forces.[7] But his 1970 study (translated into English in 1973 with the title *The Fantastic: A Structural Approach to a Literary Genre*) offered as well, and for the first time, a sustained analysis and a structuralist poetics of these narratives. He based this poetics on the concept of "hesitation" on the parts both of protagonist and reader, deriving and developing this notion from such earlier writings as Maupassant's, who already in 1883 had written that

> when men believed without hesitation, fantastic writers took no precautions in spinning their amazing tales. . . . But, when doubt penetrated men's minds, the art of the fantastic became more subtle. The writer looked for nuances, skirted around the boundary of the supernatural rather than entering into it. He found terrible effects by remaining at the limit of the possible, by throwing the souls of men into hesitation, into bewilderment.[8]

Formalizing this concept, Todorov proposed that the fantastic emerges in "that hesitation experienced by a person who knows only the laws of nature, confronting an apparently supernatural event" (25). These texts, he felt, illustrate that fragile domain, and hence fragile genre, situated *between* the marvelous (those texts in which the reader knows to suspend belief) and the uncanny (those in which a rational explanation serves in the end to explain an occurrence). They are texts that disturb not just by reason of the events they describe but for the anxiety the reader experiences in his or her uncertainty how to read those events. As Todorov insists:

> In a world which is indeed our world, the one we know, a world without devils, sylphides, or vampires, there occurs an event which cannot be explained by the laws of this same . . . world. The person who experiences the event must opt for one of two possible solutions: either he is the victim of an illusion of the senses, of a product of the imagination . . . or else the event has indeed taken place. . . . The fantastic occupies the duration of this uncertainty. (25)

Tobin Siebers's *Romantic Fantastic* (1984) added another, more anthropological dimension to our understanding of this narrative form. Concentrating on the interactions among violence, superstition, and the literary, he explored the alliance between the fantastic and Romanticism through their similar relation to the structures of superstition. Both Romanticism and the fantastic could best be viewed, he felt, as rejections of the exclusionary practices of the Enlightenment, and as exemplary uncoverings both of superstitious patterns of thought and of the logic of supernaturalism.

There appear to be no studies, however, that address what I perceive to be this form's surprising alliance with the practices of nineteenth-century realism.[9] Todorov's seminal work, moreover, for all the rigor of its structuralist approach, is often restrictive and limited. On the one hand he suggests that fantastic narrative must be viewed as part of a continuum, as a genre that is achieved each time only more or less perfectly. On the other hand his structuralist frame leads him to exclude whole categories of texts—to exclude, for example, all those in which a protagonist's possible madness destroys (in his view) any hesitation on the part of the reader in interpreting a story's events. If the protagonist is mad, he proposes, the events at hand may be rationally explained: they become the marks of an insane mind that in no way troubles the sane-minded reader. In doing so Todorov is unable to encounter as interestingly as he might the bulk of tales from Poe and from Maupassant (these, he says, merely partake of the uncanny), tales that in my view bring us closest, to the limited extent we can speak here of fixed points or boundaries, to the heart of this narrative form.

My own strongest criticism of Todorov's study lies then in the way his analysis is unable theoretically to account for those texts in which madness is significant.[10] I do not, however, begin with his analysis, or with that of any other theoretician, in an effort to depart from some established position. Indeed, I assume throughout the usefulness of his categories, while addressing in Chapter 4 his work's inadequacies. Nor do I consider such issues as the relations between fantastic narrative and the Gothic, or between fantastic narrative and the Romantic imagination, questions explored in Siebers's *Romantic Fantastic*. I have allowed my choice of texts to be guided by the corpus of "canonical" fantastic literature, as this has come to be defined, but free of it as well.[11] I have been guided by this corpus to the extent that I have wished to raise new issues in a set of texts that have, for varying reasons, been grouped together—thus my discussion of such tales as Nodier's "Une heure ou la vision," Hoffmann's "Der Sandmann," Gautier's "Arria Marcella, souvenir de Pompéi," and Maupassant's "Le Horla." But I also depart from that corpus. Poe's "Berenice," because of its "madness," would hardly satisfy Todorov's full requirements for the form. Nor, for similar reasons, would some writers place immediately within the genre, as they understand it, Balzac's "Chef-d'œuvre inconnu" (1832). A tale that is a discourse on the nature of representation itself and on the fragments that necessarily define that enterprise, it is the text that opens and closes my analysis.

In every case my approach to reading is accretive—modeled on a notion of rereading. From chapter to chapter I often reencounter tales I have discussed already, in order to explore through successive and differing lenses their significance in the larger scope of my argument. Poe's "Berenice" (1835) serves to exemplify in Chapter 2 the stark physicality of these tales' fragmented bodies (Poe's narrator's obsession with his cousin's demise ends with his horrifically pulling her teeth from her body), while Chapter 3 considers this tale's fragments for their possible production within the narrator's gaze. Maupassant's "La Chevelure" (1884) enables on first encounter a discussion of the easy exchange in these texts between animate and inanimate objects, while in another it elucidates a complex web of voyeuristic glances extending from the narrator to the madman to the asylum director to the reader. Balzac's "Chef-d'œuvre inconnu," finally, begins the book, but the last chapter returns to this text; the very fragments that had first signaled this tale's intimate alignment with fantastic narrative turn out simultaneously to be a testing of the ideals and possibilities of realism. At every point varied inter-pretation is valued for its ability to undo certain binary opposi-tions without entirely abandoning them, and to test the progres-sive steps of the argument against familiar narratives.

Throughout this work I take very seriously the fact that fan-tastic narrative is fundamentally a nineteenth-century phenome-non, a literary development to be considered as much for its si-multaneity with the realist novel as for its descent from earlier forms. Its first texts date from the last quarter of the eighteenth century with the publication of Jacques Cazotte's *Le Diable amou-reux* in 1772, but its full development took place in the century following, and most agree that by the end of the nineteenth cen-tury the form had exhausted itself.[12] Similarly, the realist novel in Europe reached its zenith in the middle to late nineteenth century, to be replaced in the twentieth century by something quite dif-ferent. Todorov already offers some insight into this coincidence when he notes that "the nineteenth century transpired . . . in a metaphysics of the real and the imaginary" (*The Fantastic*, 168). But this observation leads him to conclude that "the fantastic is nothing but the bad conscience of this positivist era" (168). He casts the fantastic as an opposition, an underside, an "other" in every respect to its realist counterpart, and here I would have to disagree. Despite the important differences between these forms—and the early chapters of this work will lean quite heavily on these—in the end the "imaginary" of fantastic narrative is un-cannily close to the "real" of the novel, its fascination with the realist's world quite striking.

Most striking, however (and from this I take my point of de-parture), is the insistent presence of bodies in these texts, and es-pecially of "bodies in pieces." The phrase is Lacan's; I use it here in its largest, most suggestive sense. As I discuss in Chapter 3, these bodies both are and are not the same as those Lacan so com-pellingly invokes in his articulation of the mirror stage and of the *corps morcelé* that attends it.[13] They are bodies that are to be seen everywhere, luring protagonists and unsettling readers. They lend their strangeness to texts that borrow their effect not from the supernatural but from the substance of some utterly familiar domain. And they are usually gendered bodies, attesting frequently to a violent, even when loving, misappropriation of the female form, violence and misappropriation that my discussion only begins to explore. Uneasy markers of a sometimes jubilant, sometimes anguished, always persistent poetics of the fragment, they link fantastic narrative—both as counterpart and as twin— to the project of realism, and to that modern sensibility so perfectly caught since that time between its romantic agonies and the compelling exigencies of an increasingly and stubbornly material world.

Throughout the book, translations are my own unless otherwise indicated. Page numbers, when cited, refer to the original source.

CHAPTER I

The Erotics of Descriptive Shattering

UNVEILING BALZAC'S
"UNKNOWN MASTERPIECE"

[Description must be governed by certain strict laws. Otherwise,] far from giving us clear and distinct ideas about the bodies that cover and compose the earth, [it] present[s] to the mind only unformed and gigantic figures, dispersed without order and traced without proportion: the greatest efforts of the imagination would not suffice for perceiving them, and the most profound concentration would fail to conceive their arrangement. . . . One would recognize, finally, only detached parts, without their unifying relationships.

—Denis Diderot, *L'Encyclopédie*

Well, I've often seen a cat without a grin, but a grin without a cat! It's the most curious thing.

—Lewis Carroll, *Alice's Adventures in Wonderland*

In a certain sense all narrative reality is a problem in emergence—a strategic uncovering, in a strategic order, of images that can only ever be partial. The writer must construct a world through the process of description in language, and to describe a thing is already to be obliged to break it into its parts before striving in the telling to reassemble its wholeness. Unlike the creative process inherent in painting, where one is limited to picturing those objects that can be juxtaposed in space, in narrative, as

Gotthold Lessing pointed out in his *Laokoon* of 1766, one may only express with certainty what is consecutive in time. As Lessing would write, the poet may render an object spatially only by first looking at its single parts and then presenting these one after another. He or she tells us only "little by little" what the painter's eye takes in with a single glance, "and it often happens that upon arrival at the final trait we have already forgotten the first" (*Laokoon*, 97).

And yet the painter's project, so different from the one of the writer, serves from some points of view to underscore the difficulties of the writer's task. During the Renaissance, artists such as Albrecht Dürer and Leon Battista Alberti often viewed their subjects through a carefully divided grid, constructed so as to allow them to see, consecutively, an array of parts. As Alberti would explain, and as we see illustrated in the well-known drawing by Dürer (see pp. 12–13), it was a thin veil marked into parallels that was

> always the same thing in the process of seeing. . . . In this parallel you [would] see the forehead, in that the nose, in another the cheeks. . . . On panels or on walls, divided into similar parallels, you [would] be able to put everything in its place. (*On Painting*, 68–69)

In similar fashion the writer must constitute images from an array of parts, moving from one small section of text to another as he or she re-creates here the model's nose, there the cheeks.

But the writer's project is also—and this fundamentally—unlike the one of Dürer's graphic artist. The writer is unable to suppress, in the final creation, a reliance all along on the fragment—on a part-by-part creation that remains ineluctably visible. He or she is faced with a kind of descriptive partialization that makes even of the narrated realist portrait a scene made up of "blocks" of meaning—"a cubist reading," as Roland Barthes would say—where "meaning is in fact a set of cubes, piled up, wedged together, juxtaposed, and yet following, each one, closely on the other's heels" (*S/Z*, 67–68).

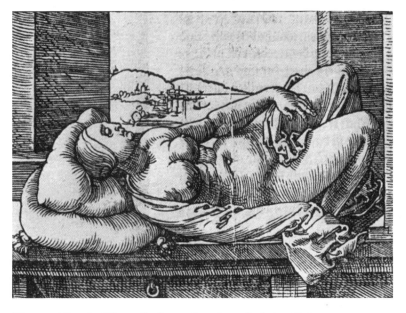

Fig. 1.1 Albrecht Dürer, *Draftsman Drawing a Reclining Nude*, ca. 1525 (The Metropolitan Museum of Art, New York, Gift of Felix M. Warburg, 1918 [18.58.3]; all rights reserved, The Metropolitan Museum of Art)

To manipulate this emergence of meaning as one uncovers the parts of an image is either to reproduce an image as we expect to see it or to transform that image into something else. One thinks of Diderot's extraordinary analysis of description, cited in this chapter's epigraph, where we read that unless description is carefully governed, "far from giving us clear and distinct ideas" it "present[s] to the mind only unformed and gigantic figures, dispersed without order and traced without proportion" (*Encyclopédie*, 4:878). Perspective may become anamorphism, "real" may turn fantastic, through the strangely *ontological* power of the descriptive process. For the literary imagination of the nineteenth century, moreover, this ontological power was of particular im-

portance. This was a century fascinated with the scopic, and with recalling a proliferating world through the very speaking of it. In science, in history, in literature, as Alain Buisine has pointed out, it was a century preoccupied with rendering the visible, a century that made of description a strategy for re-creation as much as for depiction, "a means of resurrection, even more than a manner of representation" ("The First Eye," 272).

There is a way of course in which we, as readers, conspire in the ontological power that description in language seeks to enable, and we are at our best in the realist setting. Here, despite descriptive shattering, narrative emphasis invites our vision to settle ultimately on moments of assembly, encourages us to "see" the images before us as completely as possible, as quickly as possible. When we are introduced to Vautrin in Balzac's *Le Père Goriot*, we are given not just a series of parts that describe his person, but certain broader outlines, certain unifying essences, placed in such a way as to unite his portrait into a coherent image:

> He was one of those people about which is said: "There indeed is a devilish rogue!" He had broad shoulders, a well-developed chest, muscles that showed, thick hands that were square in shape and strongly marked at the joints by thick tufts of bright red hair. His face, lined with premature wrinkles, showed signs of hardness that his supple and good-natured manners belied. His voice, . . . in harmony with his great mirth, was not unappealing. He was obliging and quick to laugh. . . . Moreover, he knew about everything— ships, the sea, France, countries abroad, business, men, events, law, hotels, and prisons.[1]

In this passage "thick hands" and "tufts of bright red hair" become the lesser details of a character who is, quite simply, "a devilish rogue." The number of things he knows, similarly, are indices of his knowing "about everything." The novel's scenes, however detailed, are ones that we remember in a visually satisfying way and as if they were the product of pure mimetic reflection. Its strategy (as I will discuss more thoroughly in Chapter 5) is to suppress our sense of the fragmentary wherever and however it can.

Fantastic narrative, on the other hand, short-circuits description as process. It becomes fascinated with isolated, constitutive moments. It emphasizes the halting stages before the picture is complete. When the narrator of Poe's "Berenice"[2] describes his ailing cousin, we are moved across the parts of her body in a way that at first recalls Balzac's description of Vautrin. But only at first: here the image we get of Berenice is one that finally draws us *away* from her person as a whole, as it focuses more and more keenly on a single part.

> The forehead was high, and very pale, and singularly placid; and the once jetty hair fell partially over it. . . . The eyes were lifeless, and lustreless, and seemingly pupilless, and I shrank involuntarily

from their glassy stare to the contemplation of the thin and shrunken lips. They parted; and in a smile of peculiar meaning, *the teeth* of the changed Berenice disclosed themselves slowly to my view. . . .

. . . Not a speck on their surface—not a shade on their enamel—not an indenture in their edges. . . . they were here, and there, and everywhere, and visibly and palpably before me. . . . In the multiplied objects of the external world I had no thoughts but for the teeth. . . . They—they alone were present to the mental eye. . . . I held them in every light. . . . I surveyed their characteristics. I dwelt upon their peculiarities.[3]

Fantastic narrative brings to life the "coming-into-view" as much as the view itself, resurrects the parts just as much as it resurrects the whole. Like Lewis Carroll's Cheshire cat, appearing and disappearing for Alice one portion at a time, fantastic narrative tantalizes its often anguished audience with its refusal to allow its images to "appear" more quickly, delights in offering an occasional, uncanny, disembodied grin.

Balzac's "Chef-d'œuvre inconnu" illustrates this phenomenon precisely. The story's protagonist, the old painter Frenhofer, works in spatially juxtaposed images, but it is the way in which he paints stroke by stroke (in a way not unreminiscent of Alberti's and Dürer's methods) that is the subject of the tale. The final realization he seeks, one that only a painter could dream of, is founded upon his fascination with the gradual application of nuance upon nuance, and this fascination makes his canvas increasingly similar to a fictional text.[4] In the last analysis his efforts resemble those of the narrative artist; his failures, those of his own narrator. The tale itself, meantime, sheds uncanny light on the way in which the fragments and partial bodies of fantastic narrative—its "catless grins"—seem at times to be the traces of representation itself.

The aging Frenhofer in Balzac's tale is an artist whose life has been relentlessly devoted to art and to art's most supreme challenges. He regrets that his master, Mabuse, died before imparting to him some final secret to artistic perfection, and yet he knows he has come quite close. His artist friends insistently wish to view his works, to see for themselves what he has described as his effort at achieving the greatest possible art, at rendering figures with such exquisite perfection and so close to life that they would almost appear to breathe the air around them—to be ready to step down from their canvas. Certainly nothing short of this will be acceptable in the case of what Frenhofer hopes will be his masterpiece, his portrait, the lovely *Belle-Noiseuse*, on which he has worked for ten full years.

As the tale opens, however, it is the fragmentary that seems to characterize every artistic project. Frenhofer informs his friend Porbus, on a visit to his studio, that this latter has fallen short of fully rendering a lovely saint. Her painted image, he explains, is wonderful in breast and shoulder, but she remains "a silhouette with only one side, . . . an appearance cut away from a larger whole."[5] Porbus's studio itself is no less a study of art in its pieces, with its myriad bits of plaster, its fragments of sculpted bodies, its "torsos of ancient goddesses" (391). Frenhofer's own master project is yet another fragment: when Porbus and the young Nicolas Poussin ask him to allow them to see the unfinished masterpiece he has carefully hidden for so long, he must disappoint them. His masterpiece, he says, is not yet complete, though often, "in the dusk" (400), it seems he has almost finished. In similar fashion, finally, the narrator fails in "picturing" for us in language the precise figure of Frenhofer, giving us merely a panoply of disparate parts: "a bald high forehead, . . . a small flat nose, . . . a mocking age-lined mouth, a short chin, . . . a grizzled beard, . . . a slim and feeble body" (390–91). The narrator can give us, as he himself will note, only "an imperfect image of this personage to whom the feeble light near the staircase further lent a fantastic color" (391). The tale seduces both reader and protagonist with incomplete images forever on the verge of an apparently desired wholeness.

But behind this tale of an artist's assertions that an image does not "live" until the final stroke has been applied is the story of the fragments that litter the path to completion and that do, ironically, come to life. Frenhofer curiously illustrates his theories on perfected, living "completion" with the example of the *hand* of one's mistress. One could succeed or dismally fail in art, he explains, already in this one part: "A hand, since I have taken that example, a hand is not just a part of the body, it expresses and continues a thought that must be grasped and rendered" (394). In a discussion of Raphael, shortly after, he claims that "Every face is a world" (395). When Frenhofer criticizes Porbus's saint, finally, insisting that "here it is a woman, there a statue, farther on a corpse" (393), there is a sense in which certain portions of the work stand, nevertheless, successfully on their own: "This place breathes, but this other is immobile; life and death battle in every detail" (393).

The most telling of the tale's fragments, however, is the one that takes us utterly by surprise at the conclusion of the narrative. In a scene that is striking for its violation of women, one in which their bodies circulate beyond their control and as the objects of a gendered and one-sided economy, Frenhofer first insists he would never allow his Belle-Noiseuse to be soiled by the look of another man, and then agrees to precisely this in exchange for a viewing of the nude body of Poussin's young mistress. This, he has been told, may inspire him with the necessary final touches to his masterpiece. Poussin, in his turn, is horrified at the thought, but then acquiesces. Frenhofer, he reflects, is a fellow artist and a great master who has promised a viewing of *his* mistress in exchange.[6]

What this bartering produces, however, is not the body of La Belle-Noiseuse but merely one extraordinary part. When Frenhofer (following his successful private viewing of Poussin's young mistress) ecstatically unveils his now-finished portrait, an astonished Porbus and Poussin are able to see only one small portion of one small foot, emerging from the corner of a canvas that has otherwise been, it seems, obliterated by a chaos of line and color. It is a fragment that is, for the reader along with Porbus and Poussin, both lovely and disappointing, fantastic (I would suggest) and exquisitely real. It is lovely because it suggests so much—because the tale has taught the reader to fill in what must accompany the part, and to be the exception to Frenhofer's anguished complaint, "Personne ne nous sait gré de ce qui est dessous" (No one gives us credit for what lies beneath; 398). And it is "fantastic" because its lifelikeness uncannily points to a perfect young woman beneath the mass of lines—points to a perfection that the text has both continually deferred but also tantalized us into believing possible. We have heard, for example, how the great Mabuse, Frenhofer's old master, fooled his king with a costume of painted paper. Why not, then, a living Belle-Noiseuse? We have seen, through the eyes of the young Poussin, the "supernatural glint" in Frenhofer's eyes, and the way some demon seems at times to move his hands fantastically and against his will (398). We have watched as Frenhofer has transformed Porbus's saint into "a new picture, but a picture drenched in light" (397). We have waited as long as the others, finally, for his long-hidden Belle-Noiseuse, and expect, with the others, that she *will* capture life completely—step down, as it were, from her canvas. We are so close to expecting this outrageous impossibility that when she does not appear in the end (or at least not to the glances of Porbus and Poussin), it is *this* that seems fantastic. The confused masses of color seem more impossible, more shocking, than if she had breathed, as Frenhofer had promised, and had risen to her feet.

Porbus and Poussin are, then, petrified with admiration for this tiny foot, but they are disappointed in their hopes of seeing the entire maiden. While Frenhofer joyfully (and mistakenly) articulates their wonder, saying, "You stand before a woman and you are looking for a painting" (411), all they see is one small fragment, appearing "like the marble torso of some Venus, emerging from the ashes of a fire-ruined town" (412).[7] The last brush stroke that was to bring her to life, the fullness that Frenhofer had lovingly sought with nuance applied upon nuance, has led only to an excess of description, to too many parts, to a descriptive process that, though strained to its limit, could neither reach completion nor avoid overrunning its mark. "Oh! nature, nature!" Frenhofer had earlier exclaimed, "who, indeed, has ever caught you in your flight! Mark well, too much knowledge, like ignorance, produces negation. I lack faith in my work!" (401).

In a spectacular treatment of this story, Michel Serres has written that *La Belle-Noiseuse* can be understood as a kind of "turbulence," an "unchained sea," a "Proteus constantly escaping"; it is an image of which "each appearance—each experience—is a luminous beacon and a veiling beacon, a brilliance and an occultation" ("La Belle Noiseuse," 35). She is neither painting, nor representation, nor work of art, he goes on to say, but "the black box that . . . buries every profile, every appearance, every representation, the work of art finally" (35). Far from being "excess," in this view, she represents instead an infinite source of originating energy. From this perspective, moreover, it becomes less clear that Frenhofer has failed. If this "escaped fragment" is as "delicious" and "alive" as Poussin and Porbus immediately think, it is perhaps exquisitely possible that there *is* "a woman beneath" (412), as Porbus suddenly cries out, and that she is as delicious and alive as this one fragment. If Frenhofer has successfully hidden her from all eyes for ten years, he may now cherish the confused lines that cover her, see in them not excess but a sheltering veil. Or, should she not be there, it may be that as a painter Frenhofer has pictured her complete, but that as a lover, and in the rhetoric of the erotic, he has needed only the perfect loveliness of her foot. Either way he may hope our judgment of perfection will take as its standard not the maiden we do not see but the foot that we do.

The glory of this tale would seem to lie not just in its insistence that there is a fullness to be reached in art, a possibility for completion that would be a "bringing-to-life," but also in its covert pleasure in the part—a pleasure cleverly disguised by its quest for the whole. As for Frenhofer's masterpiece, it may be that one, perfect piece, and "unknown" only to some. However we speculate, Frenhofer shrewdly covers his traces, leaving for his artist friends only a suggestion of his Belle-Noiseuse. Just so had Mabuse, the master painter under whom Frenhofer had apprenticed, left his secrets unknown, so that Frenhofer must exclaim at his death, "Oh Mabuse, oh my master, . . . you are a thief, you have taken life away with you!" (396). Similarly, the narrator who brings forth Frenhofer, complaining from the outset that he can hardly portray this figure, destroys *him* in the end before his picture is complete—before Poussin or the reader has had some final view. The day following that disastrous day when Porbus and Poussin don't "see" the maiden that Frenhofer has created, Porbus goes again to visit the older artist, only to learn that "he had died in the night after burning his canvases" (414). On the levels of description and of story, in the realms both of language and of paint, the images of the text remain mortifyingly partial, while the tale itself disappears in a flurry of the incomplete.

*

Conceived part by part, color by color, the creation of *La Belle-Noiseuse* becomes, in a sense, a privileged illustration of the descriptive shattering at the heart of all narrative representation. That shattering is marked with fragments as well as with descriptive excess, and both are phantasmagoric and incomplete. Both illustrate, however painterly their origin, the way in which what is seductive in language, as Roland Barthes has pointed out, are the glimmering moments where something is almost said, almost represented, where what is staged is simultaneously an "appearance-disappearance." Envisioning this as a kind of erotics and in the garb of the human body itself, Barthes writes:

> The most erotic place on the body, isn't it *that place where the clothing gapes*? In perversion (which is the regime of textual pleasure) there are no erotic zones . . . ; it is intermittence, as psychoanalysis has said, that is erotic: that of the skin that scintillates between two things (the pants and the sweater), between two edges (the open shirt, the glove and the sleeve); it is this scintillation itself that seduces, or better yet: the staging of an appearance-disappearance. (*Le Plaisir du texte*, 19)

For Barthes it is not the body that is responsible for some erotic zone. It is the clothing that covers this, that "dis-covers" the erotic moment, as in the Balzac tale it is strategic absence that highlights presence. It is what the text does not say, what it reveals through what it veils, that determines the texture of our pleasure in it.[8] One thinks of the passage in Flaubert's *Madame Bovary* where the narrator says of Emma that "her long dress got in her way, although she held it up by the skirt; and Rodolphe, walking behind her, saw between the black cloth and the black shoe the delicacy of her white stocking, that seemed to him as if it were a part of her nakedness."[9]

But where Barthes's text and the language he describes give us with one hand and take away with the other the "erogenous zones" he says don't exist, Balzac's tale allows that one small foot. Beyond and behind its play of parts and wholes this tale betrays an eroticism that is as complex as it is elusive, where it would seem no accident that the body (the masterpiece) Frenhofer hopes to complete is that of a woman, or that his final stroke should have been inspired by the negotiated glimpse he himself is allowed of Poussin's young mistress. Nor is it surprising that the one small part that survives his method (in his friends' view) should have been her foot. As I will discuss at greater length in Chapter 3, fantastic narrative is far from impartial in the objects it most delights in taking apart: morselization, here as elsewhere, is utterly bound up with the erotic, while the erotic, as Kaja Silverman has noted, is almost always cast in a feminine form ("Fassbinder and Lacan," 68–69).

The seductive play of what becomes a kind of "Cheshire effect" occurs, moreover, on more than just the descriptive plane, even when we remain solely within the domain of representation. Thus, in Balzac's tale, if the fragmented emergence of *La Belle-Noiseuse* repeats in paint the measured gestures of description, so also is descriptive partialization doubled by a certain narratological "teasing forth." Story becomes portrait as flourish is added to flourish and as the sequence of tableaux begins to create (or fails to finish) a coherent picture. Hence this tale's abortive conclusion. Hence, too, its tantalizing opening pages in which the young Nicolas Poussin is haltingly introduced, hesitating before the reader (as he hesitates before the door of the artist Porbus) like a lover "who dares not present himself at the home of his first mistress" (389). The outcome of this delay is itself postponed by a sustained panegyric to the glory of young ambition, then aggravated further by the sudden arrival of the bizarre old man whose lifework will be the focus of the tale. When the two finally enter Porbus's studio, our view of the young Poussin is again set aside. Another eight pages of text will be recorded before either of the older artists takes note of the younger, and when they do and ask his name, he replies by inscribing this at the base of one of his drawings— inscription that constitutes yet another postponement (into another mode of representation) of representation.

In a similar way Nodier's "Une heure ou la vision" (1801), another fantastic tale of the nineteenth century, reveals a pattern of partial moments and intermittent glimmerings in a way that pervades every level of the narrative, echoing some fragment lying at the center of the tale.[10] Here a narrator becomes fascinated with a young man's story, a young man he encounters one night and who appears to him only in the most gradual way. He sees him first as a shadow that "rose up before my feet," then as "an apparition," shortly after as "a phantom," and only finally as "a thin young man, all disheveled."[11] The narrator will meet the young man on several occasions, pursuing his story almost as obsessively as the young man pursues the woman he loves. In a final scene, having found his young friend dying in a hospital, the narrator learns that his friend has at last found his beloved Octavie. As the young man explains, he sees her hand reaching out toward him "at every moment" (20), and, as he speaks, the narrator himself seems to see the imprint of a hand on the pillow beside the young man's head.

This final scene is compelling for the way the extraordinary imprint is reported by the most reasonable of narrators. And it is a scene that brings together the incremental progress of three separate pursuits—the young man's pursuit of Octavie, the narrator's of the young man, the reader's of the narrator—each one coalescing into a separate portrait while also forming, together, a fragile orchestration of floating parts that mimic in their way the lovely hand whose image remains so striking at the tale's conclusion.

In Hoffmann's "Der Sandmann" (1816)—a story that produces a similar effect—a narrator reveals his anguish at having a story to tell that he can only present one portion at a time. What he would love to do, he says, would be to gather up everything into the very first word—"everything wondrous, magnificent, horrible, joyous, terrifying"[12]—and then deliver this in a single "electrical shock" (18). Instead, he says (and his metaphor is particularly apt for this discussion), he will proceed something like the portrait painter who first sketches in a few audacious strokes, then simply adds, little by little, "ever more and more color" (19).

But he finds this project an impossible one as he weaves together the several stories of Nathanael's relationship with Clara, of this latter's infatuated love for Olimpia (the beautiful robot fashioned by Spalanzani), of his encounters with Coppelius (the treacherous friend of his father who visits in the late evening to practice alchemy), as well as the story of his own (the narrator's) problematic relation to the tale he tells. All these stories, moreover, are strewn with partial bodies, as narrative shattering adds its own weight to the violence of descriptive partialization. The story of Coppelius is marked by his snorting and trampling, by his "hairy fists" (8), and by that moment when, having caught Nathanael spying one evening on his activities, he proceeds to "unscrew" the boy's legs and arms in order "properly to observe the workings of his hands and feet" (10). Nathanael calls him, later, "a black fist" (23) that from time to time was thrust into his life with Clara, while the bits and pieces that he remembers of him will return to haunt him again and again in the figure and features of the peddler Coppola.

In "Der Sandmann" and in "Une heure ou la vision," just as in Balzac's "Le Chef-d'œuvre inconnu," there is a privileging of the part that takes place as much in narrative strategy as it does in language.

*

There is a certain "bewitching, yet indescribable difference," the narrator of one of Hawthorne's tales remarks, that "always makes a picture, an image, or a shadow so much more attractive than the original."[13] It is this difference, as I hope to show in the chapters to follow, that fantastic narrative seems continually to underline, and it plays this out already at the level of representation in language. Whether in the texture of its descriptive shattering or in the effect it achieves narratologically, this literary form makes a point of the very strategic uncovering that is present in all narrative; it flaunts the unveiling rather than the veil, or some perfect picture beneath this.

It is for this reason that Balzac's tale provides an apt point of departure for a study of this form, representing as it does (uncannily) the shattering of representation itself. In doing so it signals the ways in which that shattering ever threatens to spill into other domains. And it "theorizes," in the jubilant but also horrified voice of Frenhofer, a veritable poetics of the fragment. In the end, Frenhofer's *Belle-Noiseuse* becomes not just an imaging of the narrator's descriptive efforts but also a *mise-en-abîme* of the text itself—of its dismembered limbs and its resistance to, yet desire for, incompletion. In her partial body the text records its own morselization, in her seductive parts its erotic nature, in her fragments and in her excess the fantastic. One wonders, indeed, whether the fantastic tale's discourse of the body is a discourse of the violence it performs upon itself, and its violence its most perfect moment of pleasure.

As it narrates the picturing of an unpicturable picture, as it figures the narration of an unnarratable text, Balzac's "Chef-d'œuvre inconnu" makes of itself its own almost-visible object of desire, its own unknown masterpiece: a partial body inviting, in its turn, some infinite project.

CHAPTER 2

Berenice's Teeth, Edison's Android, and the Violated, Material Body

> The teeth!—the teeth!—they were here, and there, and
> everywhere . . . before me: long, narrow, and excessively
> white, with the pale lips writhing about them.
>
> —Edgar Allan Poe, "Berenice"

It may be true that for all narrative there is no other beginning than the fragment and every description must begin with the part; in fantastic narrative this fragment often remains fragmentary, often dominates until the part has begun to eclipse its framing context. This literary form allows to remain unanchored those pieces that underlie every effort at totalization in narrative art. Its texts reveal the illusory wholeness of mimesis and its ironic dependence on a binding together of shattered parts.

There are bodies in fantastic narrative, however—the hand scrambling across the window frame, the heart beating beneath the planks—that remain in excess even beyond the partializing forces of language. What I have called the "Cheshirization" of language and of story, so perfectly emblematized in Frenhofer's picturing of the body in pieces, tends to bring with it a material shattering: what begins on the level of representation is worked out in a more tangible domain as these tales' narrators first describe in pieces, then become entranced by these, and finally allow the pieces to take on a certain power of independent life. The fragments of fantastic reality defy the requisites of fictional and lin-

Fig. 2.1 Auguste Rodin, *Assemblage of Heads of "The Burghers of Calais,"* late 1880's (Rodin Museum, Philadelphia: Gift of Jules Mastbaum)

guistic constructs. They resurrect material space despite their partial nature. They give way to a palpable confrontation with the human body itself, a body that is ultimately experienced as a vexed and often threatening set of grotesquely severed, separately functioning parts.

It is this utterly tangible body, its appearance prepared through the fragments of representation, that we most remember from these tales. After reading Nodier's "Une heure ou la vision" we recall less the partialized (because gradual) appearance of character and of plot than the hand of Octavie that beckons to the young protagonist and whose heavy imprint the narrator sees pressing itself upon the pillow. As the narrator tells us, "It seemed to me I saw the straw on which his head rested . . . become depressed beneath the weight of the hand of Octavie, and conserve its imprint" (21). In Hoffmann's "Der Sandmann" we assemble as necessary the various parts that constitute Nathanael and Coppelius, read over the piece-by-piece introduction of Olimpia's several charms. But we linger a little longer over the assortment of spectacles displayed by the peddler Coppola that, toward the end of that tale, wink and blink and stare at Nathanael, and we are disturbed to read that Olimpia's robot eyes, when she is finally ripped apart by her creators, are thrown, "bloody" against Nathanael's chest (38). Even in Hawthorne's "The Birthmark," where we learn of a husband's frantic and fatal efforts to remove from his wife's cheek a mark in the shape of a perfect human hand, what makes this tale most compelling is the way this hand (already symbolically rich) begins to appear so thoroughly material, so "hideous[ly]" distinct (166)—a "frightful object" with its crimson color (167). "Stealing forth" and "glimmering to and fro" with Georgiana's changing emotions (167), sinking down with its "tiny grasp" (168) in order to take hold of her heart (in the dream where Aylmer tries in vain to cut it from her cheek), obliterating Georgiana's cheek entirely in the photograph her husband takes of her, it is a hand that occupies fully not just Aylmer's attention but the reader's as well.

One might say this insistent promotion of the human body

in its pieces results, in fantastic narrative, in the achieving of a
kind of "supernature" within nature itself. Just as description itself has a certain potential for creating such monstrous figures
as the grotesque, "gigantic," and unhinged to which Diderot
points[1]—indeed, just as Diderot's *Encyclopédie*, as Roland Barthes
has suggested, "explode[d]" the world it sought to narrate, giving us, in its plates, the "enigmatic womb," or the bust "with the
arms cut off, the breast laid open, the face thrown back"[2]—so too
the vision of fantastic narrative seems to operate as a "division"
of the world. A tiny hand becomes hideous when it appears in a
place it shouldn't be; a single breast, a bejeweled arm, seem
strange when isolated. What is "poetic" in the *Encyclopédie* image,
according to Barthes, is the way in which it "cross-sections, . . .
amputates . . . , wants to get *behind* Nature" (1358). Fleas begin
to look like huge steel-plated dragons, snowflakes like harmoni-
ous flowers, as nature is transgressed through a "displacement of
the level of perception" (1356). In just this manner, in fantastic
narrative the real is constantly "overcome [*débordé*] by *some other
thing*" (1357).

And yet, paradoxically, this promotion of the part in fantastic
narrative would seem also to reflect a quest for unity in a world
whose wholeness has been lost to view. Walter Benjamin, in his
discussions of the nineteenth-century imagination, speaks of the
growing "commodity-like character of things," and of the way
in which "in the convulsions of the commodity economy we begin to recognize the monuments of the bourgeoisie as ruins even
before they have crumbled" (*Reflections*, 155, 162). Jean Baudrillard speaks of the disappearance of meaning following the Enlightenment, the disappearance of "the entire universe of 'Stim-
mung'" (*Système des objets*, 34). Georg Lukács speaks of a world
that, beginning with the nineteenth century, has lost its "natural
unity" (*Theory of the Novel*, 37). Our world, he says, "has become
infinitely large and each of its corners is richer in gifts and dangers
than the world of the Greeks, but such wealth cancels out the positive meaning—the totality—upon which their life was based"
(34). If to remedy this the realist enterprise would seem to have

wished to accumulate the tiniest parts in order then carefully to mold them into cohesive wholes (itself a problematic venture, considered more fully in Chapter 5), fantastic narrative may have worked toward similar ends by tolerating the pieces. It makes of *these* the independent wholes it so desperately needs as its narrators and protagonists become their own species of nineteenth-century collectors. The parts that fascinate them function to make "whole" the incomplete (to redefine the incomplete as complete). Dismembered bodies become the movable terms of personal, modifiable systems. "Real" values are lost in the end, or exchanged, in favor of a homogeneous system of signs in which such objects as the tiny hand on Georgiana's face are disconcerting both for the way they are detached from their normal places and for their perfect replication of objects we immediately recognize as whole. To collect parts of things, as Jean Baudrillard has pointed out, is to be interested in whatever is "factitious, differential, coded, systematized" in the object ("Fétichisme et idéologie," 216)—in whatever may be abstracted from this and made more perfectly malleable.

Recognizing a part as a part, of course, grows increasingly problematic—a fragment is always a whole for something smaller, a whole always a part in a larger system, and fantastic narrative exacerbates this dilemma. On the one hand it raises the specter of an infinite process of shattering; on the other, it threatens a destruction of the very possibility of the fragment. In either case its narrators and protagonists weave for themselves a world that is, in some sense, invulnerable, a world in which partial bodies begin to function as though ontologically complete.[3] As I will discuss in a later chapter, it is unity that is often at stake in these tales, sought in the wholeness of the single part—in an imagined coherence that finally, and smoothly, sutures every division.

*

But coherence, pursued through parts, sometimes leads merely to smaller parts and to a certain inevitable fetishization of the real. Poe's "Berenice" (1835) shows this particularly well. A story about loss—about the disintegration of harmony, of rain-

bows, of the mother, of youth, of meaning—this is also a story
where the nostalgic desire to return to these seems only to achieve
their further breaking apart. The narrator tells how he has suf-
fered from an extremely peculiar condition, one that seems to
have overcome him during precisely that period when his cousin
Berenice was stricken with "a species of epilepsy" (211). We learn
that he has developed a "morbid attention" to the most ordinary
objects, that this has led to an obsession with his cousin's teeth,
and that his obsession has continued unabated even following the
announcement of her death and burial. On the day after her
burial, he remembers awaking from a "confused and exciting
dream" (217) only to learn that Berenice was put living in her
tomb, that her grave was violated, that her teeth were horrifyingly pulled out, and that *he* was the author of this crime.

The tale begins with memories of far better things—of "past
bliss" and time-honored halls (209), of "aerial forms," of musical
sounds, and of a mother's "spiritual and meaning eyes" (210).
Now, however, all has somehow turned to anguish: beauty has
become "unloveliness" (209), the mother has died, and this death
would appear to have occurred in the very chamber (perhaps even
at the time) of the narrator's birth. Some state of wholeness,
whether real or imagined, has been lost, and the desire to regain
this both reverberates through and determines the narrator's
account.

We watch, for example, as the physical environment that surrounds the narrator becomes an array of fractured pieces—as,
"through the medium of [his] distempered vision," objects assume for him a "refracted and unreal importance" (212). The library chamber, marking some primal origin (for it is here where
the narrator was born, here where his mother dies, and here
where both his earliest recollections and his present story unfold),
has been reduced to its "peculiar . . . contents" (209)—to the volumes that line its walls. These books, already partial objects (since
only the sum of them composes a library), are further reduced to
their surface details as he muses "for long unwearied hours," his
attention "riveted to some frivolous device on the margin" (211),

or gives a sentence all his concentration "for many weeks of . . . fruitless investigation" (213). He has a way, furthermore, of fragmenting his heritage, for while we hear of his "hereditary . . . paternal halls" (209, 210), it is only his mother who is ever invoked, and while he reveals his baptismal name, that of his family he "will not mention" (209). As for his cousin Berenice, whose gradual "dissolution" (211) he takes great pains to follow closely, she is soon considered not in the fullness of her person but in either her moral or her physical aspect: in his "lucid" intervals he reflects on the larger picture of her tragedy, but more often he revels in the less important changes. She becomes a little like his books: promising meaning but finally determined in fact by surface detail—determined, that is, less by qualities intrinsic to her than by the force of the narrator's own reflecting.

> In the silence of my library at night—she had flitted by my eyes, and I had seen her—not as the living and breathing Berenice, . . . but as the abstraction of such a being; . . . a thing . . . to analyze; . . . the theme of the most abstruse although desultory speculation. (214)

It is no wonder that as he reflects, her body fragments into its various parts, each of these taking on a life of its own. Her yellow ringlets of hair fall about her forehead, "jarring discordantly" with her countenance. Her "seemingly pupilless" eyes are fixed in a "glassy stare." Her lips part "in a smile of peculiar meaning" while the "spectrum" of her teeth horrifyingly "disclose[s]" itself to view (215). This spectrum is quickly divided into its individual members and each of these acquires a special place in his mental life: "I pondered upon their conformation. . . . I shuddered as I assigned to them . . . a sensitive and sentient power, and, even when unassisted by the lips, a capability of moral expression" (216). As spectrum becomes spectacle (and spectacle almost spectator), the "*phantasma* of the teeth maintain[s] its terrible ascendancy" (216).

As the tale ends, fracturing and refracturing are still the rule in the narrator's constant efforts to put together, to "re-collect"

in some sense his own musings. He awakens from a disturbing
(but "exciting") dream (217), one that he can only recall as "written all over with dim, and hideous, and unintelligible recollections." He "strive[s] to decypher them," he tells us, "but in vain"
(217–18). As he struggles to gather together the dream's meaning,
a servant enters and whispers to him of a body "disfigured" in the
night (the body of Berenice, of course), a body placed "still
breathing—still palpitating" in its tomb, and then violated (218).
As the servant speaks, the narrator seems to become, suddenly,
conscious of something, and he quickly tries to grasp a little box
lying on his table. But here another breaking apart occurs. As he
reaches for the box, it slips from his hand and bursts into pieces
with a "rattling" sound (219), mimicking, perhaps, both the rat-
tle of death and the fracturing of Berenice's grave, and revealing
those teeth that have now fully become the dismembered objects
they were imagined to be.

     If this story has been read by some as the perverse tale of a
man for whom Berenice's teeth become the horrific image of his
sexual fears—a *vagina dentata*—I would add that her objectifica-
tion and reduction to parts has a far broader implication. Her
body is not just a fetishistic site that betrays a fear of castration.
It is an expression of anxiety in the face of a pervasive falling
apart—of the narrator's world, of the narrator's psyche, of the
narrator's own body. Although he has shattered the body of his
cousin, it is in fact *his* body that he has sought from the beginning
to suppress and forget. In his words, "To lose all sense of motion
or physical existence, by means of absolute bodily quiescence
long and obstinately persevered in: such were . . . [the] least per-
nicious vagaries induced by [my] condition" (212). While pon-
dering "bitterly" upon his cousin's devastation he is only too
aware of his own, insisting that it was "in the lucid intervals of
my infirmity, her calamity . . . gave me pain" (213; emphasis
added).

     In the concluding paragraphs of his narration the brutal act
that he perpetrates upon his cousin parallels, then, the way he becomes, himself, shattered, voiceless, "feminized." Here his me-

nial takes him "gently by the hand" and speaks to him in a distinctly masculine ("husky, and very low") voice, while the narrator "spoke not" (218). (Earlier, on p. 214, we had been told that Berenice "spoke no word.") When at last he manages to utter a "shriek," this too echoes his cousin, whose "shrill and piercing shriek . . . ringing in my ears" (218) had awakened him from the night's experiences. The violence done to Berenice's body and the pain it causes, finally, are strangely evoked through the physical damage done to his body: his hand, we learn, is "indented with the impress of human nails" (218), while his garments (undoubtedly like hers) are "muddy and clotted with gore" (218). Like the body of *La Belle-Noiseuse*, Berenice's body is an instantiation of the obsessive violence that lies behind the fragments on which this narrative form is built, and of the power these fragments often acquire as they usurp their framing contexts.

In the end, this is a tale both of the whole becoming the part and of the part taking on its own independent ontological wholeness. As the teeth hover before the narrator they are able not just to displace the woman to whom they belong, despite their limited form, but also to replace the narrator's own fractured form. This transformation seems to occur, moreover, on the level of the visual (we will return to this in the next chapter), for it is what the narrator sees that continually attests to what is. He is descended from a "race of visionaries" (209). He tells how when he awoke from earliest memories he "gazed around . . . with a startled and ardent eye" (210). He relates that it was while he "gazed upon her, the spirit of change swept over [Berenice]" (211). His vision seems to create his cousin as much as to mark her presence, for it is always her "image" rather than her entry that is reported: "she flitted by my eyes" (214); "uplifting my eyes, I saw" (214); "my eyes riveted upon her person" (214). "I saw [the teeth] *now* even more unequivocally than I beheld them *then*. . . . They were . . . visibly and palpably before me" (215).

More to the point, just as description is for the writer the pool of partial signifiers from which a larger picture may be constructed, so vision, for the protagonist who moves inside a tan-

gible world, is the pool of objects—often only partially signified—from which *he* resurrects for himself a certain reality. One
could say that his vision functions in a way that is not unlike description in language, or perspective in the painting of a picture.
The latter, as Jurgis Baltrušaitis points out, is a science that is not
just a fixing of the exact dimensions and positions of objects in
space but also "an art of illusion" that recreates those objects, and
whose history "is not only the history of artistic realism but the
history of a dream" (*Anamorphic Art*, 4). The protagonist's vision
is always only ever *simulating* wholes and can be exposed in this
effort with the slightest deformation in the point of viewing.
What he sees is always disparate until his judgment narrates its
parts, always limited—a synecdoche for the reality he "envisions." However widely he may try to focus, it is an unorga-
nized text from which to surmise, and then to build, a larger
context.

As with language, moreover, one can hardly step outside this
perceptual realm. "If all men, in the place of eyes, had green
glasses," as Kleist wrote in 1801, "they would have to conclude
that the surroundings they perceived through these *are* green.
They would never know whether their eyes presented to them
objects as they are, or whether instead something *was added* to
these, something belonging not to the objects, but to the eyes"
(*Sämtliche Werke und Briefe*, 2:634). Just as the rhetoric of description problematizes representation in language in the leap it requires of the reader for getting from part to whole, so vision
problematizes perception when it requires of the viewer a leap
from what is seen in fact to what is not seen. Whether in Kantian
terms or in Cartesian ones (for both philosophers those objects
that we think we see with our eyes we really only comprehend by
our mental power of judgment),[4] that faculty we most associate
with truth and literality turns out to have its own particular creative power. Available prior to description, it is a form of representation—a "rhetoric," in a sense, for the tangible world—the
"language" before language with which we tell ourselves stories.

There is a way, then, in which the narrator in Poe's "Berenice" sees not less well but only differently. One could argue that he sees more "literally" than the rest of us. In the intensity of his meditations he chooses to maintain the parts: he prevents his judgment from making the leaps that constitute "normal" reality as he muses for long "unwearied" hours, his attention "riveted to some frivolous device on the margin"; he becomes absorbed "for the better part of a summer's day, in a quaint shadow falling aslant upon the tapestry" (211); he finds in the teeth of his cousin enough to occupy his entire viewing. His vision next to ours, like fantastic description next to that of realism, is an unmasking of device and a "making strange" of the consequent picture.

*

If to partialize the world in the realm of the material body allows the real to be "overcome by some other thing"; if it is a way in which unities that have been lost may be further fractured until the fractures begin to constitute new unities; if it is that moment in fantastic narrative where the playful images of descriptive resurrection are exchanged for a kind of "literal" vision, it is also a process through which bodies (as bodies per se) and objects (as objects) are radically, often irretrievably, blurred.[5] This occurs because partialization on the literal level operates with metonymic energy more than that of the metaphor, producing displaced parts that are vulnerable to successive changes in their ontological status. We see this displacement in "Berenice," where the spectrum of teeth is produced through a moving away from the whole to which it belongs, though movement away, in this particular case, is achieved through magnification. As the narrator explains, at the termination of his reveries "the first cause [of his meditation], so far from being out of sight, . . . attained [a] supernaturally exaggerated interest" (212). The whole, it seems, is obliterated through the sheer intensity of the part's outline.

In a similar way the literal breaking apart of the House of Usher, in the tale by Poe in which a narrator witnesses the final demise of the Usher family, is produced through a kind of lateral contagion and displacement. Indeed, if the house in this tale has often, and rightly, been viewed as a metaphor for the brother and sister who inhabit it—if it has been neglected and soon will fall, as will these last representatives of the Usher family—it is also true that its "body," though it is very much like theirs, has borrowed from them incompletely and will owe its final demise, as I will discuss below, to the instability of a more metonymic exchange.

One cannot, of course, separate as neatly as one might wish the workings of metaphor and metonymy. Maria Ruegg points out that

> the rules for semantic replacement are nothing but abstractions (metaphors) for the rules of syntactic displacement. . . . [There is] a constant and inevitable mimetic *play* between a multiplicity of codes, texts, contexts: play which implicates *all* discourse in a complex, ambiguous, undecidable web. ("Metaphor and Metonymy: The Logic of Structuralist Rhetoric," 146)

Gérard Genette, in his "Métonymie chez Proust," similarly shows the necessary coexistence of the two tropes in any descriptive moment. But Genette allows one to imagine the two tropes as distinct, even if simultaneous, saying, "only the crossing of a metonymic thread with a metaphoric chain assures coherence, the 'necessary' cohesion of the *text*" (60).

Using that distinction, I would distinguish between the *principally* metaphoric dynamic at work in this tale and the more metonymic one that functions, simultaneously, beside it. In the domain of metaphor, just as brother and sister have floating gray hair, hair of "more than web-like softness" (402), so the house has a gray sedge and minute fungi "hanging in a fine tangled webwork from the eaves."[6] Just as brother and sister wander vacantly, eyes perhaps bloodshot with fatigue, so the house has "vacant and eye-like windows" that are "long, narrow and pointed," and through which "feeble gleams of encrimsoned light" barely glimmer (401). The Ushers' silken hair grows "all unheeded" (402), just as the house's gray stones are in a "crumbling condition" (400). The "enshrouded" figure of Madeline, alive and breathing as she approaches the narrator's chamber at the end of the tale, is replicated in the way the mansion, at that moment, is "enshrouded" with a "distinctly visible gaseous exhalation" (412). Just as this brother and sister reflect and complete one another (they are twins, we learn), so the house is perfectly duplicated in the muddy tarn that surrounds it, where "inverted images" reflect horrifically its own "gray sedge, . . . [its] ghastly tree-stems, and [its] vacant and eye-like windows" (398). Indeed, just as Roderick and Madeline seem throughout this tale the two inadequate halves of a split consciousness, the house is fractured in two with its "barely perceptible" zigzag fissure (400).[7]

But the force of this metaphorical relation is undermined by metonymic energy, as certain attributes seem to leak in partial fashion from player to player, rather than to be reflected whole. If Roderick and Madeline are almost identical, if they share "sympathies of a scarcely intelligible nature" (410), yet they also share parts that can only belong to one *or* to the other. Thus the narrator can never view the pair in a single glimpse: when he first sees Madeline he quickly looks at her brother, only to find this latter covering his face with his hands. Roderick Usher, meantime, as though imagining his sister as an embodiment of some part of him that has somewhere in the past been lost, envisages, in the poem he writes, a monarch whose glory, now only "dim-remembered," once "blushed and bloomed" (407). Indeed, with Madeline's apparent decease, Roderick loses entirely any balance he might have had and begins to acquire deathlike features:

> His ordinary manner had vanished. His ordinary occupations were . . . forgotten. He roamed from chamber to chamber with hurried, unequal, and objectless step. The pallor of his countenance had assumed, if possible, a more ghastly hue—but the luminousness of his eye had utterly gone out. (410–11)

Similarly, when it mimics not just their floating hair and "enshrouded" figures but also their "fissure," the house of Roderick and Madeline Usher reproduces the essence of brother and sister as well as their incompleteness—the impossibility of the one ever fully (safely) reflecting the other. They seem to have a continuing effect on it (its fissure grows to fatal proportions by the end of the tale) just as truly as it has affected them—just as truly as, for Roderick, "some peculiarities in the mere form and substance of [the] family mansion, had, by dint of long sufferance, . . . obtained [an influence] over his spirit" (403).

If we are tempted, then, by this and other tales to speak of the literalization of the metaphor, we must speak as well of that metaphor's metonymical violation. The House of Usher does not just metaphorize the violent death of its inhabitants, it helps to bring it about as it enters into their exchange, as it shares in their "sympathies," as it draws its own portion from their store of limited energy. Hence their destruction, as Madeline's body falls in "upon the person of her brother," and as the walls of the house, with "a long tumultuous shouting sound," rush asunder (416, 417).

In both "The Fall of the House of Usher" and "Berenice" originating wholes are not left intact; there is an exchange of parts that can never be a complete exchange. While the metaphor allows our judgment to move between signifier and signified with ever richer and more complete correspondence, here there are often equally powerful partial reflections, and parts breaking off to function independently. Berenice's teeth, the House of Usher itself, all those parts that float so freely through the pages of these tales are violations of the living bodies they represent so incompletely.

But if, through the metonymies of partialization, the body in Poe is often turned to object (Berenice's teeth are, simply and fatally, catalogued as *objects* of interest within the narrator's world), in Théophile Gautier's "Arria Marcella, souvenir de Pompéi" (1852) and in Guy de Maupassant's "La Chevelure" (1884) we find instead the object taking on all the attributes of the human body. In Gautier's tale the narrator describes the hills surrounding Pompeii as though each were an erotic site, noting their "undulating" and "voluptuous" lines—"like the hips of a woman."[8] The walls of certain ancient women's apartments appear to him, with their faded colors, like cheeks "from which the makeup has been imperfectly wiped" (245). The tale's protagonist—the young Octavien—finds himself enthralled with an ancient remnant of hardened ash in which he finds clearly embedded the imprint of a perfect breast. "Arria Marcella" is a text filled with partial images like these that hover between body and object, from the ashen imprint with which the tale begins, to the small table supported on griffin's feet, to the "splendid phallus" placed above most of the stalls in Pompeii in order to ward off the evil eye, to the single white hand that reaches out to Octavien from a passing carriage, beckoning him on.

Maupassant's "La Chevelure" (a text I will discuss both here and in the next chapter) provides an even more stunning example of this blurring of objects with bodies. "One merely looks at an object," the "madman" tells us, and, "little by little, it seduces you, troubles you, invades your consciousness as would the face of a woman. Its charm enters into you, a strange charm that comes from its form, . . . from its physiognomy as an object; and one loves it already, one desires it, one wants it."⁹ (One wonders whether all things that "seduce, trouble, invade one's consciousness," are destined to do so "as would the face of a woman.") The madman (whose first-person narrative is relayed to us by the narrator) pities those of us who are ignorant of that "honeymoon of the collector with the knickknack he has just purchased" (109–10). He spends hours upon hours gazing at an antique watch, wondering what hand might have held it and turned it and polished it "at the tips of its warm [*un peu chauds*] fingers" (108). He notices how clearly the watch still lives and breathes: "It hadn't in any way ceased to throb, to live its mechanical life, and it continued still its regular ticktock" (108).

But his attraction to objects is most fully described in the case of one particular dresser, a lovely sixteenth-century item that he sees one day and finally must purchase.¹⁰ He "adores" it "with a lover's tenderness," he is "ravished" by it, he tastes with it all the "intimate joys of possession" (110). One night, after careful investigation, he discovers its secret drawer and succeeds in forcing this open with (significantly) a small knife that he inserts into a crevice of the woodwork. He finds there, against a background of black velour, a wonderful mesh of a woman's hair, the odor of which (though now, indeed, the odor is of the dresser) leaves him stunned: "I stood there utterly stupefied, trembling, troubled! An aroma almost imperceptible, so old that it seemed the soul of an aroma, floated up from this mysterious drawer and from this surprising relic" (110).

Material object in this tale is, on the one hand, still material object: the antique watch has its "mechanical life," its "regular ticktock." But that ticktock is a kind of heartbeat; the watch "throbs." As for the dresser, it hides a mesh of hair that in the past belonged to a real woman but that now, certainly, is the dresser's *own* most exquisitely developed, most womanish feature. Object has become body with all the necessary intimate accoutrements, absorbing perfectly the libidinal charge cast upon it. Indeed, just as the body of some original female is violated when the narrator appropriates, for the dresser, the hair that once made her beautiful, there is violation done as well to the body of the dresser, a body that has been gendered female. It too is fragmented and fetishized: it is encountered erotically, explored according to its parts, and with the discovery of the mesh of hair its larger structure falls away. The madman now finds in this the fullest achievement of his dreams, shuts himself up alone with it, sinks his teeth into it, is enervated "to malaise" (112).

Object, moreover, is "body" here, in the further sense that Gaston Bachelard has explored in his *Poétique de l'espace*, according to which wardrobes with their shelves and desks with their drawers are "veritable organs of the secret psychological life." They are "hybrid" objects, he says, "subject" objects. "They have, like us, through us, for us, a quality of intimacy" (83). The dresser is not just "other," with its outer forms and its textures to be touched, but also self, with its inner spaces reflecting the inner in ourselves. On both counts it becomes the body's subtler form, a perfect locus for reinvesting meaning, and an interesting twist on what Lukács has called the nineteenth century's "dissolution of the human . . . into the not-human.'"[11] The unfamiliarity of the environment is transformed here into the "familiar" body; the very marks of external disorder become, phantasmatically, their own solution. The "disorder" of objects becomes a "system" of objects (to use Baudrillard's term)—"imaginary solution to contradictions of every order" (*Système des objets*, 183). Lost intimacy re-emerges, if with a new, material aspect, in a form that is both hopeful and terrifying.

*

Nowhere, however, is there a more complete, more complex blurring of bodies with objects than in Villiers de l'Isle-Adam's spectacular *L'Eve future*, a novel that, for all its length, does not contradict the contention that fantastic narrative prefers not just fragmented, incomplete moments but also forms that are less totalizing than that of the novel.[12] Divided into six books, each of these split into ten to twenty separately titled two-to-three-page sections, *L'Eve future* unfolds like a series of prose poems. As the tale opens we find Edison, the noted American scientist, musing in his private laboratory, receiving a telegram and dropping this casually among his things, only to notice the way it alights on the most curious of objects—it falls into the grasp of a beautiful bejeweled severed arm, as this lies quietly on its velvet cushion. It is a human arm, we are told, "placed on a cushion of violet silk,"[13] around whose delicate wrist a viper, studded in gold, winds itself. On one finger sparkles a ring of sapphires. Its perfect fingers hold a pearl-colored glove. Its skin is firm and satiny. Its flesh is of a tint so alive that "the impression it gave was as cruel as it was fantastic" (45). The narrator notes an area of congealed blood and a few purple drops on a rag beside it that seem to indicate "a recent operation," and wonders what "unknown hurt" could have necessitated this "desperate amputation." Indeed, the "healthiest vitality" still seems to flow "in this sweet and gracious specimen of a young body" (45).

We will learn, eventually, that this "human arm" (45) is in point of fact absolutely inanimate, another victory in Edison's repertoire of inventions. But we are invited to forget this each time it reappears in the story. Its lifelikeness is utterly perfect, its

drops of blood are just "barely . . . clotted" (45), its satiny skin
contrasts completely with the artificial trappings woven about it.
Indeed, the ebony table, the cushions of violet silk, the enamel
viper, the sapphire ring, the pearl-colored glove (that "must certainly have been donned many times"; 45) only serve to highlight
its own difference from these artifacts. It is an arm that exudes
ontological fullness, so compellingly does the blood seem to flow
in its veins, so gracefully do its fingers hold an elegant glove as
they catch the missive Edison has just received, so calmly do the
eyes of the bracelet snake, wrapped about its wrist, "observe"
their inventor in the obscurity. It is an arm that is a fitting introduction to a novel filled with female bodies—both living and not,
both wakeful and somnambulent—whose parts seem ready at
every moment to circulate with perfect deception.

The missive caught in its grasp, we learn, turns out to be a
message from an English gentleman by the name of Lord Ewald
who is on the verge of suicide in his frustration at loving an exquisitely beautiful but unintelligent woman. He has come to
Menlo Park to pay one last visit to his good friend Thomas Edison, who is dismayed to learn of Ewald's plans and unable to talk
him out of them. Edison does succeed, however, in convincing
his friend to postpone his suicide until such time as Edison might
give to him a perfect replacement for the object of love that has
been so disappointing. The replacement he has in mind is a lovely
android on whom he has worked for some time, and who, with
certain final touches inspired by Ewald's real mistress, he hopes
will not only replicate the beauty of that more disappointing love
but will provide in addition "spirit" and "intelligence" (38, 101).

In the android Hadaly (for this is what Edison calls his creation) one sees already the easy reduction in this novel of bodies to
objects and to circulating parts. In a passage that is as horrific as
it is fascinating, Edison reveals how, at the touch of one of her
rings, her "feminine armor" conveniently opens up as she lies on
a table before him (170). Edison soberly observes (to the chagrin
of Ewald) that Hadaly may be subdivided easily into four parts.
She is composed, first, of an "interior System" that includes "her

Equilibrium, her Gait, her Voice, her Gestures, her Feelings" (171). Then there is her "plastic Mediator . . . a sort of armor with flexible articulation" (171). Her body is, thirdly, penetrated by an "animating fluid" that gives her her "Carnation." And she has a human skin that governs not just her coloring but even "the vividness of her Smile" (171). Hadaly's talents are similarly extraordinary, similarly disparate, and similarly suited (as Edison implies) to a gentleman's needs: when she is finished, he explains, she will sing as beautifully as Hoffmann's Antonia, will be as passionately mystical as Poe's Ligeia, will have the seductive powers of the Venus of the musician Richard Wagner, and will think in the words of the greatest of thinkers. All this and more will have been carefully prerecorded on two golden discs inside her (99).

But Hadaly's is not the only body to circulate through the pages of Villiers's novel. We are confronted as well with the disjointed nature of Alicia Clary, Lord Ewald's disappointing English mistress, whose body and mind, as Edison puts it, are not just disproportionate but absolutely in disparity. We see it in the divided body of Any Anderson, a widow and Edison's friend, whose powerful grief has left her in an incurable, unbroken state of sleep, and out of whom Edison is able, by means of the science of "electromagnetism" (101), to generate a separate "speaking self." We see it in this other self of Any Anderson, a self that is so fully realized (out of Any Anderson's body) that it will become a partner to Edison, will carry on with him an ongoing communication, and will call itself by its *own* name: Sowana.

But in many ways the most fully partialized body belongs not to Alicia or to Any Anderson or even to the android Hadaly but to the seductive Evelyn Habal, who before the story begins has driven to suicide the erring husband of Any Anderson. Here is a woman—studied by Edison, of course, and captured, for his better analysis, in moving photography—whose entire being is the product of the highest artifice. Without her arsenal of makeup and varied devices, he explains, without her scarves, her belts, her radiant synthetic hair, her pots of facial colors, her special eyelashes, her luminous false teeth, her ointments, her embellishments for satiny skin, her nail polish and high heels, without the corsets that make perfect her every contour, she is merely (or so Edison says)

> a little anemic being, vaguely feminine, of stunted limbs, of hollow cheeks, of toothless and almost lipless mouth, with a head nearly bald, with eyes lusterless and beady, with drooping eyelids, [and] with a wrinkled body, entirely skinny and dull. (161)

"Made up" or nude, Evelyn Habal adds to the novel her own special fund of floating parts and divided identity, parts that seem bound to circulate. Just as Mistress Anderson allows her sleeping body to be the encasement for "Sowana"; just as Sowana gives her voice to Mistress Anderson as this latter sleeps unaware, and later gives her spirit to Hadaly (this, indeed, will be the spiritual portion that so perfectly completes, and brings to life, Hadaly's robot body); just as Alicia Clary seems to have borrowed, for *her* beauty, the *Venus Victrix*, while also allowing her own borrowed beauty to be the mold for the body of the robot Hadaly, Evelyn Habal "puts on" and "takes off" her parts according to whim.[14]

There is something, of course, more than disturbing in Edison's "dissection" of Evelyn Habal. It points to all the dissections in the novel and betrays both misogyny and naive idealism. Edison is shocked by her artifice, and uses it to describe the deception of which a woman is capable, all the while creating, himself, an android whose deceptive origins make of her, he thinks, the positive pinnacle of art and of science. The women in the novel become so many Galateas, each one more or less "complete," each one more or less deficient, each one an object of unsettling display, so that Edison enjoys viewing Hadaly's impressive mechanical organs with the same relish with which he mocks Evelyn Habal's stunted, "anemic" being. His "dissection" of Evelyn Habal's and of Hadaly's appearance only further underlines the way in which, as Laura Mulvey and Colin MacCabe have noted, the female body "has become industrialized":

> A woman must buy the means to paint on . . . and sculpt . . . a look of femininity, a look which is the guarantee of *visibility* in sexist

society for each individual woman. Advertisements sell the means of production of the look, sealing it in with the mark of feminine desirability, attainable by means of lipsticks, bras, scents and so on—magic formulae depending on novelty for appeal just as the market depends on turnover for profit. Magazines provide the know-how . . . , sealing the association of *woman* and *sexuality* in the minds of women themselves. It is almost as though woman herself were a factory, . . . painting on the mask and emerging transformed with value added in the process, a commodity ready for consumption. ("Images of Women, Images of Sexuality," 54)

If what makes *L'Eve future* so extraordinary is the mysterious spirituality that ultimately characterizes Edison's android, a spirituality generated somehow from the body of Any Anderson, a spirituality that even Edison doesn't quite understand, this is so because it is *in* this spirituality that Hadaly finally defies her audience, in this spirituality that she escapes their Pygmalion grasp, in this spirituality that the novel redeems itself from an otherwise relentless crush of violent dismemberment.

This novel's circulation of physical bodies is carried out, finally, even narratologically, where we find each body inscribed in someone else's narration. The narrator, in his "Advice to the Reader" (29), tells us of Edison, while Lord Ewald tells Edison of Alicia Clary. Alicia Clary, within Ewald's narration, tells him of herself, and then Edison tells Ewald of Edward Anderson. Following this, Edison tells Ewald of Hadaly, of Evelyn Habal, and of Mistress Anderson, and how, in his sessions with the last of these, Sowana told him of herself. The consequence of this circulation is a symphony of deception that only further confuses the confusion of bodies with objects already present within each character. The ever-sleeping Mistress Anderson is juxtaposed with Sowana while Sowana drifts between Anderson and Hadaly. Evelyn Habal is, on the one hand, pure feminine seduction and, on the other, "Artifice alive through illusion" (167). Alicia Clary hovers precariously between the *Venus Victrix* she so unnaturally resembles and the statue of her that Edison promises will dazzle actresses to come. Hadaly, finally, somewhere between life and death, body and object, human and robot, is both android and the height of "human" naturalness, so that, at one point in the novel, Lord Ewald will be unable to say with certainty to whom (or to what) he speaks. As Pierre Citron points out, she is not "an inferior, derisive, monstrous, more or less demonic caricature" of her human model: "She is infinitely superior . . . and it is her model [Alicia Clary] who is truly her caricature."[15] Everything becomes interchangeable when not indistinguishable, right down to Edison's offer, in the creation of Hadaly, to exchange reality itself with illusion, "chimera for chimera, sin for sin, smoke for smoke—*why then not?*" (213).

But *L'Eve future* is not just a story of deceptive resemblances. Even in this tale of androids there is a rejection of metaphor. In metonymically determined fashion, and in ways that recall precisely the dangers of lateral contagion evident in Poe and in Maupassant, Hadaly is *not* the same as the lovely Alicia but a violation of her model. This "Ombre," as Edison likes to call her (99), this "Shadow," fully lives up to the name, projecting like some rebellious other only her model's outline. Though she replaces Alicia with "monstrous" perfection,[16] she replaces her parts without their governing wholeness, duplicates only the deficient (and partial, in this case) physical body of her human model. Thankfully for Ewald she is no more identical to Alicia Clary than Edison's night light (his *veilleuse*) is identical to natural light, and in both cases the difference is crucial: it is only by that particular light that this *grand électricien* contemplates the severed arm at the opening of the novel, just as it is only in Hadaly's difference—in her failure to duplicate her model—that she will become beloved. As Marie-Hélène Huet has noted, Hadaly "overcomes Lord Ewald's final reservations . . . precisely *because* she is not Alicia Clary; there is a depth in her dark eyes which, in its very deceptiveness, is more fascinating than the living singer's compromised beauty" ("Living Images: Monstrosity and Representation," 81).

Hadaly's victory, however—the victory she wins in the stunning sixth book of the novel in which, despite her mechanical origin, she wins over both Lord Ewald and the reader with magical eloquence—is short-lived. This wonderful, seemingly indestructible woman robot is lost at the end of the novel on her way to Scotland with her now-joyous partner, and in a fashion that seems cruelly unfair. Her one traveling requirement—the need to be transported during sea voyages in a special coffin in the baggage compartment—keeps her from being saved along with the other passengers when a fire suddenly engulfs the ship. A broken Lord Ewald informs Edison of the disaster, after which Edison returns to work on other projects only to find that Any Anderson (the somnambulent body out of whom he had induced the spirit Sowana) is dead. As he puts down her lifeless hand on discovering her silence, he is struck again by the inanimate hand still lying on the table. In this story of robots and of replacement, of the blurring of objects with bodies and of life with its simulation, we are left with this severed arm, still so vital in its appearance, still lying in the obscurity, a grim contrast indeed to the "wholeness" of Hadaly that might have been.

*

Baudrillard has suggested that each time we personalize an object, each time we make it into a source of security or equilibrium, we become vulnerable to the underlying threat of its failure. It is a failure, he says, that we both want and don't want. We build this into its very structure as though some final defect were as necessary to our satisfaction as the object's "almost" perfect functioning—as though we needed the object to fail, at times, in order that it not surpass the imperfect self that controls it:

> The failure of an object is always perceived in an ambiguous fashion. *It undermines our sense of security, but it also materializes the objection that we continually have in regard to ourselves, and this also demands satisfaction.* We expect of a cigarette lighter that it will always work, and yet we know, even desire perhaps, that it won't work every time. . . . Infallibility always ends by provoking anguish. (*Le Système des objets*, 186)

One thinks of that interesting moment when Edison's messenger, on speaking to a wigmaker who is to make a wig of hair for Hadaly, insists that while that wig should be so perfect it might be said to compete with nature, yet one must be careful: "Above all don't do BETTER than nature!!! You would surpass your goal! *Identical!* Nothing more" (236).

It is telling, from this perspective, that Hadaly, otherwise indestructible, is lost at the end of Villiers's novel because of the trivial fact (trivial imperfection) that she is required to travel in a baggage compartment on ocean trips. The ultimate failure this occasions is not untypical in fantastic narrative. In Hawthorne's "The Birthmark" Georgiana dies when her husband tries to remove the tiny hand that mars her cheek; in Poe's "The Fall of the House of Usher" the truncated exchange between the Ushers and their mansion proves fatal; in Maupassant's "La Chevelure" the mesh of hair is taken away when the "madman" is found out; and in Hoffmann's "Der Sandmann" Nathanael throws himself fatally from a tower when he again sees the eyes of Coppelius. Whether for reasons similar to those suggested by Baudrillard, or because fantastic narrative is doomed from the beginning not to find new unity through the pursuit of parts, the fragmented body that fantastic narrative records is rarely successful.

In this failed outcome, the partial bodies that we find in this narrative form need to be distinguished from the fetish. I have spoken of a kind of "fetishization" of the real—the way in which the protagonist's world in these texts, when it is excessively contemplated in its pieces, begins finally to shatter irretrievably. And it is clear that female bodies, viewed in parts, carry at every moment a particularly heavy fetishistic load, whether it is Berenice's teeth, or the foot of La Belle-Noiseuse, or the exquisite mesh of hair hidden in the madman's dresser. Like the fetish, finally, the isolated part simultaneously completes and replaces an offending partial picture, is a sign of and a guard against partialization. Fantastic narrative, as I have tried to suggest, often makes of its pieces the coherent wholes it ostensibly banishes, just as the fetish "remains a token of triumph over the threat of castration."[17]

And yet the fetish, as Freud saw clearly, is quite successful in what it sets out to do. It is only the *part* that it seeks to replace, and the fetishist is able to find and refind this in a successful, metaphorical sort of gesture. The fetish becomes itself a perfect metaphor,[18] a part that fully "replaces" another part, and this with a mobility that allows desire, since its primordial object is never reached, to be perpetually sustained. The fantastic partial body, by contrast, would seem to be its violated, metonymical version. "Violated," because it is produced not voluntarily and in a controlling manner but as a fragment to be endured and undergone. "Violated," because it is some whole that the part sets out to replace—already a precarious venture. And "violated," because that whole could only ever hope to be realized through continuous, contiguous sliding. All movement is cut off instead, frozen and demobilized at the very moment the part itself is literally severed from the body of its host. When the crimson hand is removed from Georgiana's face, the teeth from Berenice, the mesh of hair from the dresser, Edison's android from her laboratory, La Belle-Noiseuse from behind her veil, then metonymy is derailed, the whole is lost, and the fantastic fragment left unable to reduce the anguish that produces it. Frenhofer's fears had been only too true, all those years when he had refused to reveal his masterpiece, all those years when he had insisted, "What! show you my creature, my wife? tear the veil with which I have so chastely covered my happiness? But that would be a horrible prostitution! . . . She is mine, mine alone, she loves me" (407).

CHAPTER 3

In the Haze of the Gaze; or,
The Politics of Peeking

In our relation to things, inasmuch as this relation is constituted by the way of vision and ordered in the figures of representation, something slips, passes, is transmitted, from
stage to stage, and is always to some degree eluded in it—it
is this that we call the gaze.

—Jacques Lacan, *Les Quatre concepts*
fondamentaux de la psychanalyse

Behind every real object, there is an object dreamed.

—Jean Baudrillard, *Le Système des objets*

In the last chapter I proposed that in fantastic narrative the
body's fragments often take on a distinctly material weight despite their origin in language. They become the concrete, literal
markers that most occupy the protagonist's world and that we as
readers most remember. I would add to this that in these tales of
predominantly first-person narrators, the narrator's act of looking further contributes to the body's constitution and dismemberment. It functions in collusion with the fragments of descriptive and narrative shattering as it brings the literal piece to life,
shapes the form the fragment will take in the tangible world, and
determines whether that fragment will become a thing to be
feared, desired, appropriated, or destroyed. The fragmented
body in these tales is often produced through a kind of textual
energy—through what I called in Chapter 1 the "Cheshirization"

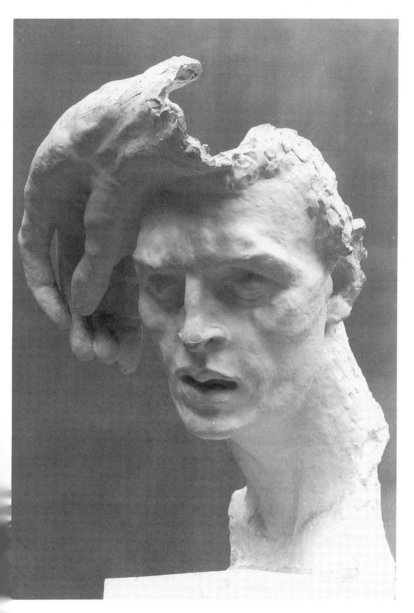

Fig. 3.1 Joseph Bernard, fragment of *Le Fardeau de la vie* (The burden of life), 1897 (photograph courtesy Fondation de Coubertin, Paris; reproduced by permission of the Bernard family)

of language and of story. But it is also the product of a gaze that both captures its visible contours and creates these anew. It is a body generated in language—in narrative strategy and descriptive technique—and it is simultaneously the expression of the vision of a particular narrator, whose act of looking translates the objects seen in particular ways.

One could say that every literary text is an invitation to a voyeur's enterprise, constructing as it does a frame around the image and activity of some other as it stages for itself and for us a particular view. But fantastic narrative appears to push this enterprise to its logical extreme. Its views never quite escape the ongoing dynamics of the "being-viewed": already and inevitably partial, they are further shattered, further "read," further filtered through some more-than-keenly interested field of vision, and there is something that is undisguisedly erotic—even scandalous—in this. In the "haze" of the narrator's vision the fragments we find in these texts register, in the end, both literal and figural meaning, and register, I suggest, both self and other. We are confronted with a mechanics of displacement: with shattered female bodies that keep redounding back upon the bodies of agonized men—shattered bodies that may in fact be the misleading signs of a fundamentally fractured masculine self. They are bodies that would seem to attest to a certain aggressive, phantasmatic voyeurism ("voyeurism" because the text itself, along with the protagonist, is always "peeking"—maintaining the part rather than seeking the whole; "phantasmatic" in the protagonist's transformation of that part into something else, whether from body into object, object into body, or, as I have suggested, from male body into female). They are bodies, finally, that reflect in narrative what John Berger has seen in European oil paintings of the nude, where the principal protagonist is in fact the spectator, presumed to be a man, standing in front of the picture: "Everything is addressed to him . . . [and] must appear to be the result of his being there. It is for him that the figures have assumed their nudity . . . [while] he, by definition, is a stranger—with his clothes still on" (*Ways of Seeing*, 54).

The bits and pieces of Berenice are most telling, then, when thought of as reflected through, or as the refracted product of, the vision of her cousin/narrator as he "reflects" upon her. Their dispersion is not only witnessed but also produced by that other's shattering energies; the horror and delight of *his* body are increasingly present to us as he violently, and determinedly, analyzes hers. As the narrator minutely relates the morbid details of a world and a woman falling into smaller and smaller parts, his complicity is clear, though his view unfolds quite innocently. It is not simply that "while I gazed upon her, the spirit of change swept over [Berenice]" (211); rather, she fragments before him precisely *because* he watches, because he holds that gaze. There is an aggressive intentionality in the look that sees her form, as the narrator "sink[s] back" passively into his chair, his eyes "riveted upon her person," his "burning glances" "[falling]" upon her face (214–15).

In the same way La Belle-Noiseuse, in Balzac's "Chef-d'œuvre inconnu," is not more centrally the point in that story than the acts of looking that create (and de-create) her image in their own particular light. Nor is her body the only one in this tale whose unveiling is charged with the special energy of some expectant viewer. At the opening of the story we watch as Frenhofer peeks in at Porbus's painting of a saint, insisting that were he to place his hand on her breast he would find it as "cold as marble" (393). He is concerned with the painting's lifelikeness, yet his critique betrays his expectation that a perfect picture also return "perfectly" (submit perfectly to) his desire. Later we learn that Frenhofer is to be the only other man to view the naked body of Poussin's lovely mistress, a favor that is itself granted in exchange for a view of *La Belle-Noiseuse*. In every case there are at least two viewings (or three, if we include the reader's view): while Frenhofer disparages Porbus's painting of a saint, Poussin stands reverent before it; at the unveiling of Poussin's mistress, Frenhofer's delight in the lady's perfection contrasts with her lover's realization that he himself hasn't properly seen her; and when *La Belle-Noiseuse* is revealed, Frenhofer is joyous, while his artist friends can only wonder at what it is he sees. The story closes with Frenhofer's suicide and with the burning of all his paintings, ensuring there will be, in the end, only visions of *La Belle-Noiseuse*, with which to reconstruct the tale.

There is a way, however, in which all these visions—each of these separate looks—combine to construct a *single* gaze, one that surrounds the body of La Belle-Noiseuse even as it emanates from her, and one that hovers with all its conflicting energies somewhere between the text, its characters, and our reading. Lacan suggests, in his *Les Quatre concepts fondamentaux de la psychanalyse*, that the gaze is not coincident with the eye of a single viewer, or even with that of a group of viewers. It issues instead "from all sides."[1] It is a "play of light and opacity" (90) that is, for the subject, "unapprehensible" (79)—an intersection of fields that form together a kind of luminous "labyrinth" (87). "What determines me most profoundly in the visible," Lacan writes, "is the gaze that is outside. It is through the gaze that I enter into the light, and from the gaze that I receive its effects" (98). (One could almost locate here a principal source of the hesitation, to use Tzetan Todorov's term, that we feel in the course of reading Balzac's tale. As we struggle to interpret what happens—what appears—in that extraordinary moment in which Frenhofer unveils his masterpiece, we are as desirous to "see" the body of La Belle-Noiseuse as any of her admirers, and just as unable to see it. There is no uncomplicated point of view from which to read.)

Maupassant's "La Chevelure" illustrates the creative power and sinuous construction of this gaze with even greater complexity. For here there is a layering of looks that seems to contaminate even our act of reading, however true it may be that, strictly speaking, reading and looking are not the same thing. (Might one imagine the act of reading as a seeing at second remove, a seeing already imbued with another's vision?) "La Chevelure" is the tale of a madman who most enjoys the objects he collects when he

imagines those unknown glances that must have adored them in
the past as he does now; of a narrator who is fascinated by the
madman's tale as this unfolds before him in the form of the madman's journal; of an asylum director who simultaneously moni-
tors the madman's shrieking and the response of the narrator as
this latter, visiting the asylum, reads the madman's journal. It is
a tale, finally, where our own reading of the narrator's account
perilously joins the one of the narrator himself, as he "reads" the
madman. Our reading completes a textured circuit of glances
from within which emerges the madman's prized "mesh of hair,"
the *chevelure* that becomes, itself, an appropriate metaphor for this
text's entangled network of gazes.

The story opens as the narrator looks into the madman's cell,
observes the grim condition of this "ravaged man" (107), and
then imagines the way in which his folly must be eating his body
bit by bit "like a piece of fruit by a worm" (107). Already, he
notes, this has left the limbs dry, the chest caved in, the belly
sunken. The narrator then proceeds to pick up and to read the
madman's journal (he is invited to do so by the asylum director)
and finds there a tantalizing account of the madman's love for objects, of his discovery of the beautiful *chevelure*, and of the pleasure this has come to provide. Most interesting, he will, at the end
of his reading, desire to see for himself that mesh of hair. Full of
emotion, inspired by what he calls his horror and his pity, and
betraying his own bodily involvement in the "view" he has en-
joyed, he stammers out a request to know what has become of
the madman's *chevelure*. The director finds this for him, tosses it
in his direction, and as it flies toward him "like a golden bird"
(113) the narrator shivers to feel its light, caressing touch. He is
left, "his heart beating with disgust and desire—with disgust as
though at the contact of objects dragged through crimes, with
desire as though in the face of temptation for a thing both repugnant and mysterious" (113).

One wonders what exact crimes inspire the narrator's disgust—the madman's, or his own in reading (experiencing) those

of the madman, or indeed, those of the asylum director, whose own act of looking captures the "look" of both the madman and the narrator. But it is clear that the scandalous part that had been all the madman needed in order to be "obsessed," "haunted," "happy and tortured" (112), provides a similar thrill, though at one remove, for the narrator himself. The madman's "madness" would appear to be dangerously contagious: the long, pleasurable shiver (the *frisson*) his body registered each time he felt the touch of the *chevelure* is fully recalled in the narrator's own shiver when, as the narrator says, "I shivered on feeling, against my hands, its light and caressing touch" (113). It is a shiver that takes its power from a reading that is no longer passive—that has trespassed upon the look of the madman as the madman has gazed at the *chevelure*. The narrator might just as well have flinched at the touch of the journal as at the touch of the coveted mesh of hair (reading and touching almost lose their difference—they begin to appear equally productive of erotic sensation), for it is more surely *this* object, in the view it provides, that has laid the ground for his disgust and for his desire. In either case, as the asylum director will say at the end of the tale, "The mind of man is capable of everything" (113).

Whether *chevelure* or journal, the object is partial, contributing to its seductive charms and ensuring that it will be, in the words of the narrator, "repugnant and mysterious" (113). Not only is the part enough to complete the picture, anything more would be too much. When the madman asks, "Wasn't it strange that this mesh of hair should have remained thus, while not a particle was left of the body from which it took its life?" (111), we suspect he might more accurately have insisted that its partial nature provides, precisely, his greatest pleasure.

The look of the madman is, of course, more practiced, more ardent than the one in which the narrator indulges, for it is bolstered by a "look" that he imagines, which provides its own voyeur's pleasure. He relates in his journal how he often used to think about that "unknown hand" that must have fondled, "at the tips of its warm fingers" (108), the very objects he now holds, and about the eyes that must have admired them. In the case of one tiny watch he wonders what woman might have worn it on her breast "in the warmth of her clothing" (108). When he finds the mesh of hair, he invents scene after scene that might explain who might have cut the hair prior to sealing it up into the marvelous dresser. Could it have been, he muses,

> a lover, on a day of farewell? a husband, on a day of vengeance? or perhaps the one who had herself worn them on her forehead, on a day of despair?
>
> Was it at the hour of [her] entry into a cloister . . . ? Was it at the hour of nailing her into the tomb, the young and beautiful corpse? (110)

Interestingly, the scenarios he imagines (the views he constructs for himself and to which we and the narrator are made privy) often narrate someone else in the act of viewing. In the case of the watch, he asks what eyes have "spied" its surface as they awaited "the cherished hour, the divine hour" (108). With the mesh of hair he imagines the bereaved lover who might have kept this one last part of the woman he loved as something "he could still love and caress, and kiss in the fury of his grief" (111). Or he sees himself in imagined past scenarios, remarking at one point, "It seemed to me that I had already lived before, that I must have known this woman" (111).

If, as the madman tells us, the past attracts him and the present horrifies him because the future "is death" (109), there may be a way in which it is his own body that is most keenly at stake in these scenes, and his fears in regard to this the basis for his need to own the bodies he imagines.[2] "Warmed to life" by his own warm breath and touch (112), his artifacts offer symbolic relief from an anguished desire to halt all movement of time—to prevent its taking from him, with each passing second, "a little of myself for the nothingness of tomorrow" (109). They offer relief, that is, from a desire to escape both his mortality and his own fragmented nature. Finally, indeed, he will push this anxiety and compensatory desire so far that, as he ecstatically announces, he will "rediscover" the whole. Having caressed the *chevelure* all night with particular passion ("warmed" it with kisses that made him "faint with happiness"; 112), he suddenly realizes that the single mesh of hair has become an entire woman—that "la belle Morte, l'Adorable, la Mystérieuse" has come back (113). "Yes, I saw her," he proclaims triumphantly, "I took her, I possessed her, just as she was when living formerly—tall, blond, fleshy, her breasts cold, her hip in the form of a lyre" (112–13).

Beyond the madman's act of looking, and beyond the looking of the narrator, is the "look" of the reader who repeats (as he or she enters into) those of the other two. The narrator's text becomes for the reader yet another journal to be perused, and one to which he or she adds the gaps and pieces of his or her own act of reading. As Roland Barthes writes, our "avid desire for knowledge leads us to skim or pass over certain passages . . . in order to find most quickly the scintillating anecdote" (*Le Plaisir du texte*, 21). We are like the spectator at a cabaret who, "stepping up onto the stage, would hasten the dancer's striptease by quickly removing her clothes, *but in order*, that is to say: respecting on the one hand, and precipitating on the other, the episodes of the ritual (like the priest who would swallow his sermon)" (21).

It would seem to be true that some texts promote more profoundly than others the reader's complicitous involvement. Novel reading, for example, as D. A. Miller writes,

> takes for granted the existence of a space in which the reading subject remains safe from the surveillance, suspicion, reading, and rape of others. Yet this privacy is always specified as the freedom to read about characters who oversee, suspect, read, and rape one another. It is not just that, strictly private subjects, we read about violated, objectified subjects but that, in the very act of reading about them, we contribute largely to constituting them as such. We enjoy our privacy in the act of watching privacy being violated, in the act of watching that is already itself a violation of privacy.[3]

In similar fashion fantastic narrative takes to the extreme principles true for all narrative and for every act of reading, capitalizing on those that play into its own particular project. The reader's act of looking is not different, in these texts, from what it must be in the face of others so much as it is more acutely drawn, more self-consciously involved. The titillation it invites, moreover, if not more erotic, is often more violent. The reader's looking is not a sharing of another's vision that encourages a kind of forgetting of one's own place and of one's own body. It is a sharing in the process producing the view—a gazing at the gaze itself.

Thus, in Balzac's tale we look with Frenhofer, or with his artist friends, rather than at *La Belle-Noiseuse.* And in Maupassant's "La Chevelure" we enter into a veritable maze of mirrored readings, each one a looking at some previous look. In Poe's "Berenice" we are invited to analyze with the narrator the form and parts of his ailing cousin, to share in the moments of, the very looking at—in his words, the "riveting of"—her person. In a very real sense the reader's body completes, either passively or aggressively, the text's/narrator's voyeuristic project. It becomes, through a kind of displacement from the text, through the sort of "contagion" that strikes the narrator of "La Chevelure," the locus for a newly erected imaginative hierarchy—yet another active viewing, if of a different sort, at one further remove. In our sharing in the gaze we participate in the sensation of the body looking, becoming ourselves bodies (with sensation) looking. Once again the asylum director in Maupassant's tale seems inadvertently to have provided an appropriate observation when he says to the narrator that the latter will find the madness of the madman, as it is expressed in the madman's journal, "pour ainsi dire palpable" (palpable, so to speak; 107).

Narration itself, finally, seems to enhance the force of the gaze so powerfully evoked in these texts. I suggested in Chapter 1 that description in language, through its very ability to slow down or to accelerate, helps to create the pieces that in fantastic narrative become independent objects rather than constituent parts. So narration (especially in the case of the madman as he recounts the scenarios he imagines he sees) reproduces and effectively draws out the desire that is reported through it. In the passage where the madman describes how passionately he loved the *chevelure*, for example, his own accelerating pulse is mimicked in a narrative expressiveness that seems itself, with its plethora of verbs, out of breath: "I shut myself up alone with it to feel it against my skin, to sink my lips into it, to kiss it, to bite it. I entwined it about my face, I drank it, I drowned my eyes in its golden wave in order to see the day blond through it" (112). When he is holding back, on the other hand, waiting for his emotions to build to greater pitch, his text betrays, appropriately, a halting staccato, especially in its repetition of the word "and" and in the use of the simple past. Thus, as he says, "It seemed to me that it [*elle*] began to move, and I replaced it on the velour dulled by time, and I pushed back the drawer, and I reclosed the dresser, and I went out into the streets to dream" (111).

In the end the madman, through "envisioned" looks, has enhanced the touch that he will then enjoy, just as that touch (for the asylum director, the narrator, and the reader) is enhanced by the journal's own exquisite narration. Together they make for the *chevelure*'s violation as a piece and for its transformation into a whole.

*

Fantastic partialization, to the degree that it is the product of a particular gaze, comes about because the look that produces some emerging object works so perfectly in concert with the process that narrates that look. The *chevelure* (like Berenice's teeth and Frenhofer's Belle-Noiseuse) is not a given, not a static point of contemplation, but a partial body actively incarnated in the text. It is "produced" by the madman from the loins of a dresser, re-encountered voyeuristically by the asylum director and the narrator (as these two unwittingly confirm and repeat the madman's view), and encountered yet again by the reader, while narration provides the transformative energy—the momentum, the suspense, the rhythm—behind this.

The importance of this "incarnation," and the degree to

which it might have been otherwise, may be seen when we contrast what happens in this tale (and in the fantastic) with what happens to an identical partial body in a text of another genre. In a lyric poem by Baudelaire, also entitled "La Chevelure" (1861), we find a mesh of hair operating just as centrally, and just as erotically, but here it is less a product of a particular gaze, or of a particular narration, than a point of departure for a reflection into the poet himself—for a contemplation that leaves the *chevelure* behind. Its partial nature is crucial, but this would seem to precede the text in order to provoke within it a reflection on the poet (on his partialization) and away from the reader:

O toison, moutonnant jusque sur l'encolure!
O boucles! O parfum chargé de nonchaloir!
Extase! Pour peupler ce soir l'alcôve obscure
Des souvenirs dormant dans cette chevelure,
Je la veux agiter dans l'air comme un mouchoir!

La langoureuse Asie et la brûlante Afrique,
Tout un monde lointain, absent, presque défunt,
Vit dans tes profondeurs, forêt aromatique!
Comme d'autres esprits voguent sur la musique,
Le mien, ô mon amour! nage sur ton parfum.

J'irai là-bas où l'arbre et l'homme, pleins de sève,
Se pâment longuement sous l'ardeur des climats;
Fortes tresses, soyez la houle qui m'enlève!
Tu contiens, mer d'ébène, un éblouissant rêve
De voiles, de rameurs, de flammes et de mâts:

Un port retentissant où mon âme peut boire
A grands flots le parfum, le son et la couleur;
Où les vaisseaux, glissant dans l'or et dans la moire,
Ouvrent leurs vastes bras pour embrasser la gloire
D'un ciel pur où frémit l'éternelle chaleur.

Je plongerai ma tête amoureuse d'ivresse
Dans ce noir océan où l'autre est enfermé;
Et mon esprit subtil que le roulis caresse
Saura vous retrouver, ô féconde paresse!
Infinis bercements du loisir embaumé!

Cheveux bleus, pavillon de ténèbres tendues,
Vous me rendez l'azur du ciel immense et rond;
Sur les bords duvetés de vos mèches tordues
Je m'enivre ardemment des senteurs confondues
De l'huile de coco, du musc et du goudron.

Longtemps! toujours! ma main dans ta crinière lourde
Sèmera le rubis, la perle et le saphir,
Afin qu'à mon désir tu ne sois jamais sourde!
N'es-tu pas l'oasis où je rêve, et la gourde
Où je hume à longs traits le vin du souvenir?

(*Œuvres complètes*, 25–26)

Ecstatic fleece that ripples to your nape
and reeks of negligence in every curl!
To people my dim cubicle tonight
with memories shrouded in that head of hair,
I'd have it flutter like a handkerchief!

For torpid Asia, torrid Africa
—the wilderness I thought a world away—
survive at the heart of this dark continent . . .
As other souls set sail to music, mine,
O my love! embarks on your redolent hair.

Take me, tousled current, to where men
as mighty as the trees they live among
submit like them to the sun's long tyranny;
ebony sea, you bear a brilliant dream
of sails and pennants, mariners and masts,

a harbor where my soul can slake its thirst
for color, sound and smell—where ships that glide
among the seas of golden silk throw wide
their yardarms to embrace a glorious sky
palpitating in eternal heat.

Drunk, and in love with drunkenness, I'll dive
into this ocean where the other lurks,
and solaced by these waves, my restlessness
will find a fruitful lethargy at last,
rocking forever at aromatic ease.

Blue hair, vault of shadows, be for me
the canopy of overarching sky;
here at the downy roots of every strand
I stupefy myself on the mingled scent
of musk and tar and coconut oil for hours . . .

For hours? Forever! Into that splendid mane
let me braid rubies, ropes of pearls to bind
you indissolubly to my desire—
you the oasis where I dream, the gourd
from which I gulp the wine of memory.[4]

Unlike the madman's (narrator's, reader's) body in the tale by
Maupassant, here the poet's body is not secretly implied, *not hiding behind* and creating the pieces of the other which then might
play the primary role. Rather, the poet's body is clearly present,
effacing the body the poet purports to be considering as he makes
of the *chevelure* the convenient "oasis" where he is able to
dream—as he makes of it the "gourd" where he "gulp[s] the wine
of memory." As he agitates the *chevelure* in the air "like a handkerchief" the poet thinks of his spirit swimming on its perfume,
of his soul drinking at its sparkling port, of his head plunging
into its dark ocean while his hand inseminates rubies and pearls
in its heavy curls. If there is a body dismembered here, it is that
of the artist himself, whose hand we see more than the *chevelure*
as it dips into the luxurious curls, whose head plunges into its
"ocean," whose spirit is caressed by its waves and swims in its
perfume. As Leo Bersani suggests, the artist in Baudelaire's love
poems "is intrinsically an unanchored self. The energy with
which he penetrates the world (or is penetrated by the world) sets
him afloat among alien forms of being" (*Baudelaire and Freud*, 15).

In both Baudelaire's poem and the tale by Maupassant the dynamic behind the subject's (narrator's) look is crucial. But in the
poem the object is all but lost in the heat of the subject's looking,
while in the tale that object becomes only more and more firmly
outlined. This difference holds even when one compares the tale
by Maupassant with the prose version of Baudelaire's lyric

poem—the prose poem entitled "Un Hémisphère dans une che-velure" (1857). Here the lyric gaze is narrativized but still reflects the same inward direction, the same subordination of the *cheve-lure* to the viewing subject. Its fifth paragraph (of seven, corre-sponding to the poem's seven stanzas) is typical. We shift from any contemplation of the hair itself to a contemplation of the body and memories of the poet, who finds ecstasy in these, and invokes their image, as he caresses the hair:

> Dans les caresses de ta chevelure, je retrouve les langueurs des lon-gues heures passées sur un divan, dans la chambre d'un beau navire, bercées par le roulis imperceptible du port, entre les pots de fleurs et les gargoulettes rafraîchissantes. (*Œuvres complètes*, 253)
>
> In the caresses of your hair I recapture the languors of long hours spent reclining on a couch in a fair ship's cabin, rocked by the im-perceptible rolling swell of the harbor, in between the pots of flow-ers and the cool water jugs.

The *chevelure* becomes almost physically present for us in the first line of the final paragraph when the poet considers biting into its heavy tresses. But in the line that follows, that very tangible pres-ence is quickly lost. The *chevelure* becomes instead, and once again, a vehicle for a new departure into the poet's memories, with the words: "When I gnaw your elastic and rebellious hair it seems to me I am eating memories" (253).

In Baudelaire the partialized body is only one among many possible sites for the poet's metaphoric imagination. It functions to "set afloat" some subjectivity that becomes then *itself* the prin-cipal object of the lyric or prose poem. In fantastic narrative, by contrast, that same body is to the end the privileged, determinant space. Here, the metaphorical quickly melts into the literal, the narrator's look "steps back" in the very face of the shattered body it helps produce, while that body becomes the endpoint of the discursive enterprise.

Still, and no less than with Baudelaire's poetry, in reading fantastic narrative one must pay attention not just to what is pro-duced but to the origin of its production—to the look, or multiple looks, through which we as readers are allowed (or forced) to see the picture framed. I have suggested (and will return to this shortly) that the narrator's look may function as a form of denial—an anguished look away from his own body and its falling apart. This would certainly appear to be the case in "Berenice," where the anguish expressed is entirely the narrator's, while the body dismembered is his cousin's. This would seem to be the case as well in Maupassant's "La Chevelure." Here the madman (in his own status as narrator of his journal) hopes to establish his body as a unity—to be able to say, "*My* body, unlike those others, is whole"—by concentrating all his energies on the morselized objects and bodies he sees all around. In both stories, the fact that those other, fragmented bodies are female is only the more convenient. This serves to keep them at a greater distance—as others that might just stay in their place.

The politics of such aggressive dismemberment would seem to change, however, when we focus on the look returned—the one of the body that consumes and contemplates the narrator in its turn. What do we do with the "look" of the phantasma of teeth, in "Berenice," that "maintain[s] its terrible ascendancy" (216)? Or with the eyeglasses that "wink and blink" at Nathanael in Hoffmann's "Der Sandmann"? How do we read the look of the old man, in Poe's "The Tell-Tale Heart" (1843), whose eye so unbearably torments the narrator? And how is this look different for being generated by a body that is, in this case, masculine? *Which* look do we read, indeed, in this story where the "vulture eye" of the old man reflects (in a double sense) both the narrator's eye and the "eye" of the lantern as these latter spy upon it for seven consecutive nights? And where the narrator returns the look of that eye when it isn't looking, allows a "single thin ray" of light to fall upon it,[5] just as that eye had so often "fallen upon" the narrator? Could one say that this is a particularly clear instance of Lacan's notion that numerous looks all inevitably combine to produce a gaze that is not coterminous with the eye of a single viewer—a gaze that is, instead, a kind of luminous "labyrinthe"? (See my discussion on p. 54.)

Or is there only ever a single eye, a single look refracted into several? Is there room within the vision the narrator shares with us for any other vision at all, let alone any participation by things perfectly immobilized, perfectly silent, perfectly dismembered? In the intensity of the looking performed by these narrators do we find instead, as we would in Baudelaire, what Jean Baudrillard (in a more general discussion) has called the "collecting-eroticizing" of the subject himself? Might one say that behind the subject's presumed discourse with the other, "the real signified is no longer the beloved, but the subject himself in all his narcissistic subjectivity, collecting-eroticizing himself, and making of the relation of love a discourse to himself" (*Le Système des objets,* 141)?[6]

Certainly, the great advantage in seeing some other from a distance, or in its parts, is to be free in this way to "re-make" that other anew—to fill in its gaps or to define its nature according to some single piece as this piece best completes or reflects (the better to attract or to terrify) one's own body. The blue eye of the old man becomes an eye that, in its act of looking, reflects the frightening intensity of the narrator's own look; Berenice's teeth must be owned, her cousin says, in order to "restore [him] to peace" (216). And yet, if it is not possible, as Leo Bersani notes, "to describe an object without wishing to devour and appropriate that object," neither may it be possible to do so without "oneself being devoured by the energy of that appropriation."[7] Looking in these texts becomes not just a vehicle of appropriation but a terrifying form of aggression, both inward and outward, and the literary text a violent imagining of other interwoven, violent imaginings. One thinks (leaving the literary) of the chilling testimony of Jeffrey Dahmer, arrested in Wisconsin in 1992 for the murder and dismemberment of seventeen young men, who murdered his victims not because he was angry with them, or because he hated them, but because, he said, he "wanted to possess them permanently."[8] As he dismembered their bodies and stored their parts, "excitement, fear, pleasure [were] all mixed together." It was a way "of remembering their appearance, their physical

beauty," since he "couldn't keep them there with me whole."
When he went so far as to set up altars with their skulls and skel-
etons and to eat their hearts after killing them, it made him "feel
they were a part of me."

Self and other become, in Dahmer's case as in these texts, perilously fused. As Jean Laplanche has noted in his discussion of
Freud's "A Child Is Being Beaten," "*Introjecting the suffering object,
fantasizing the suffering object, making the object suffer inside oneself,
making oneself suffer:* these are four rather different formulations,
but our practice shows the subject constantly moving from one
to the other" (*Life and Death in Psychoanalysis*, 97).

*

> We're each of us made up of some cluster of appurtenances.
> What shall we call our "self"? Where does it begin? Where
> does it end? It overflows into everything that belongs to us—
> and then flows back again.
>
> —Mme Merle, in Henry James, *The Portrait of a Lady*

One wonders, finally, what connection there might be between the viewing of parts that occurs in these texts as these parts
enter the light of a central gaze, and the vision of the very young
child before the child has come to know either its own body as an
entity separate from the bodies it sees, or the bodies outside its
own as more than a chaos of parts and organs. This earlier mode
of viewing the world, in Lacan's conception, is characteristic until
the child passes through what Lacan will call the "mirror stage"—
that extraordinary moment in the development of every human
psyche in which the individual recognizes his "specular image"
in a mirror, gaining for the first time a sense of the "total form"
of his body (*Ecrits*, 94–95). I am not suggesting that the images
of the fantastic are a return to this earlier mode. This early vision
of the child (a vision we can only, of course, imagine) is one entirely lacking in point of view, in privileged perspective: not only
is the child's own body (until it coalesces into a vision of wholeness) a matter of pieces, the parts the child sees all around him are
themselves lacking in any particular phenomenological center.
The gaze in fantastic narrative, by contrast, makes of point of

view, and the ostensible difference between self and other, something to be carefully, even neurotically (if not always successfully)
maintained.

And yet in that earlier world (described by Freud, Karl Abraham, and Melanie Klein, as well as Lacan),⁹ where self and other
are perpetually lost, and where there seems to be what Edmond
Ortigues has called "a never-ending play of reflections" (*Le Discours et le symbole*, 205), there would surely be room for the kinds
of images we see in fantastic narrative. One could almost hy-
pothesize a certain memory of that earlier blending of parts, and
blending of self with other, brought back in these texts by the
very creative process that finds itself exploring all the rich possibilities of the body experiencing its relation to other bodies. The
possibility of such a memory would certainly be suggested by
certain reported fantasies in dreams and in schizophrenia of the
body in pieces, of mutilation, of castration, and of the doubling
of the self.¹⁰ Thus also, perhaps, the lengthy song that Mr. Rogers, of the children's show *Mr. Rogers' Neighborhood*, sometimes
sings, with the comforting refrain: "Everything grows together,
because you're all one piece."

Indeed, and for Lacan, the "memory" of one's body as fragmented is all the more powerful for being fabricated retrospectively and from a position of imagined wholeness. If the child, he
suggests, gains for the first time (somewhere between the age of
six and eighteen months) a sense of the total form of its body in
that dramatic moment when it recognizes as whole its specular
image, yet that recognition is a very brittle one, alienated and
alienating from the beginning. It launches the individual into a
realm that is always mediated by desire for the other. And it
launches a memory of a body in its bits and pieces—a "corps
morcelé"—memory that is suddenly frightening and that is in
large part the mark of a retrospectively imagined lack of totality.
It is a lack that was not felt in early infancy but that is generated
instead from the very fragility of that wholeness the self would
seem to have acquired. And it is a lack that often manifests itself
in dreams "of disjointed limbs or of those organs represented in

exoscopy, growing wings and taking up arms for intestinal per-
secutions" (*Ecrits*, 97). The mirror stage, Lacan insists, occurs
from within the symbolic order, is reconstructed from a position
within language. As Jane Gallop puts it, "What appears to precede
the mirror stage is simply a projection or a reflection. There is
nothing on the other side of the mirror" (*Reading Lacan*, 80). One
thinks of those enigmatic words of the narrator of "Berenice"
when he says at the opening of that tale, "Either the memory of
past bliss is the anguish of to-day, or the agonies which *are* have
their origins in the ecstasies which *might have been*" (209).

It is as though the gaze in fantastic narrative were a recaptur-
ing, or a reworking in literary form, of that portion of our experience that normally remains buried and "untranslated," covered as this is by the clearer, linguistically ordered world of the
adult. It would combine a vision characterized by too little point
of view with one characterized by too much; it would be a gaze,
strangely, of both the most innocent and the most perverse na-
tures. To use, again, the terms of Lacan, the images of the fantastic would render both the realm of the Imaginary (that order
characteristic of the mind of the infant and dominated by images
of identification and duality, but built on chaotic noncoales-
cence)[11] and of the Symbolic, where concepts and language, and
the other as different from oneself, transform and overlie the images of the register that precedes it.[12]

If finally (as Fredric Jameson has suggested, using Lacan's
terms as I have above) the literary text might be thought of as a
recording of the "mastery and control" of its image content[13]—
of the sedimenting of its images and their transformation from
the Imaginary into the Symbolic—fantastic narrative would seem
to mark the misdirection of this process. Jameson's excellent discussion, which aims to recuperate certain of Lacan's theoretical
positions for a more general theory of literature, emphasizes that
only by grasping images in literary texts as "that trace of the
Imaginary . . . which has undergone the sea-change of the Symbolic, can criticism . . . recover a vital and hermeneutic relationship to the literary text" ("Imaginary and Symbolic in Lacan,"

376). The implication, however, is that that "trace" is not really traceable, that we get only what has already fully undergone the "sea-change"; here, however, the texts we are reading allow us to observe this process in the making, to catch it before it is complete. Its images are most suggestive when thought of as not fully "sedimented," not completely transformed into the more comfortable register in which we are accustomed to think and to see. If anything, they would appear to constitute a reversal of that process, one in which the energies of the narrator's vision (and of the gaze in which this partakes) strip away, little by little, the Symbolic nature of things as whole and as other, until these attain, instead, a kind of "Imaginary" status.

Hence the progression of terror in the images of "The Tell-Tale Heart," a tale in which a narrator becomes obsessed with being rid of the offending eye of a mild old man. For it is a story in which the eye that offends does so only more and more as the tale proceeds, while becoming simultaneously, and less and less, the eye of any particular person. On the eighth night of the narrator's vigil against it, as he directs his lantern's light upon it, its presence succeeds in obliterating all else:

> It was open—wide, wide open—and I grew furious as I gazed upon it. I saw it with perfect distinctness—all a dull blue, with a hideous veil over it that chilled the very marrow in my bones; but I could see nothing else of the old man's face or person: for I had directed the ray as if by instinct, precisely upon the damned spot. (795)

The narrator's concerns, however, turn soon after from the eye of the old man to the old man's body, and this body seems very quickly to become confused with his own. The narrator knows too intimately what he imagines to be the other's fright—becomes himself that other's body in his analysis of its anguish: he knows the sound of the old man's terror to be the one that "many a night . . . welled up from my own bosom" (794). He knows, he says, when the old man stirs, that the latter has in fact been awake since the very first noise, that "his fears [have] been ever since growing upon him," that he has been "trying to fancy them causeless, . . . saying to himself—'It is nothing but the wind in the chimney,'" but saying this "all in vain" (794). He knows, he says, just what the old man feels: "It was the mournful influence of the unperceived shadow that caused [the old man] to feel—although he neither saw nor heard—to *feel* the presence of my head within the room" (794). The difference between the two bodies is fully collapsed, finally, at that point where the narrator is agonized by the very beating of the other's heart: "I knew *that* sound well, too" (795). As it beats, making a sound "such as a watch makes when enveloped in cotton" (795), it incites his fury just as the eye had done, until he is forced to murder the old man, and dismember and bury the corpse.

The very maleness of the old man's body brings it too close to the narrator, makes of it a too fragile (an all-the-more unsuccessful) site of displacement. As for the old man's eye, it is as threatening as any partial body could be, "embodying" as it does the very thing (the look returned) that these narrators are least prepared for. As Beth Newman notes, "To be the object of the gaze—to be spectacle instead of spectator—is to lose one's position of mastery and control—in short, to be emasculated" ("The Situation of the Looker-On," 1032). Neither the spectacles that wink and blink at Nathanael in Hoffmann's "Der Sandmann" nor Berenice's spectrum of teeth that so horrifically "maintains its terrible ascendancy" usurp spectatorship from the narrator or protagonist viewing them so easily or so thoroughly as does this old man's eye. (Indeed, it *must* be some other part of Berenice that horrifies, in the tale by Poe that bears her name, because *her* eye would be unthinkable: "If the woman looks," Stephen Heath writes, "the spectacle provokes, castration is in the air, the Medusa's head is not far off; . . . she must not look, is absorbed herself on the side of the seen"; "Difference," 92.) The terror that begins in "The Tell-Tale Heart" as the "pale blue eye of the old man," which becomes a "vulture eye" and then a "damned spot" separate from the old man's body, becomes in the end a beating heart whose "muffled" sound is nevertheless too audible, too "tell-tale," too inseparable from the one beating in the narrator's own chest.

Again, contrary to Jameson's suggestion, the images of the fantastic (and this however they are gendered) seem to become for their narrators and for the system that narrates them not more "mastered" and "controlled," but less and less so. They may be incarnated by the text, but they also resist from the beginning those textual energies that would fully enclose their meaning, would fully recuperate their precise value. Articulated in the words of the adult, yet betraying, somehow, the perception of the child, they are bodies and parts—the hand scrambling across a window frame, the teeth hovering before the narrator of "Berenice," the heart beating beneath the planks—behind whose literal force lies some figurative meaning bearing testimony to a deeper viewpoint.

It is precisely here, in this "double" vision of fantastic narrative—in its production of value, for any given image, from both linguistically ordered and visually "disordered" energies—that I find the locus for what I called in the last chapter the violation of metaphor and of metonymy. For the retrieving of some earlier, "lost" vision, a vision now endowed with the point of view of the Symbolic subject, seems to create metonymies that are in violation of metaphor—metonymies that confuse one body with the next, one part with another, some part with the whole. Thus, for example, the eye of the old man is confused both with the eye of the narrator and with that of the lantern; the heart of the old man becomes the narrator's heart; the teeth of Berenice replace Berenice herself. At the same time these very metonymies would seem, themselves, to short-circuit: the Symbolic subject is still "subject" to the Law, and as such will take great pains to interpret the part, to recuperate its value for a larger picture, to give it a place in the fullness of an often "realistic" setting, to stop the blending, to cut off its movement (as I suggested in Chapter 2), to force it to persist radically in a single form. In the subject's desperate effort not to acknowledge any other meanings, the part becomes literally fixed—a thing to be viewed and loved (the foot of

La Belle-Noiseuse, the hand of Octavie), to be possessed (the mesh of hair, the foot of La Princesse Hermonthis in Gautier's "Le Pied de momie"), or to be despised and removed (Berenice's teeth, the old man's eye, the crimson hand on Georgiana's cheek).[14]

Despite the careful distance most often maintained in these tales between viewer and viewed, the gaze that bridges that distance continually offers its own possibilities for confusion. Berenice's teeth are, on the one hand, simply and literally, "thirty-two small, white, and ivory-looking substances" scattered, at the conclusion of the tale, across the floor (219). But they are longed for "with a frenzied desire" (215), dreaded as they float about "white and ghastly" (215), desperately needed if the narrator is ever to be "restore[d] . . . to peace" (216), because their shattered reality marks, not so literally, the shattered, displaced, misplaced psyche of the narrator himself. The dissolution of Berenice's body appears increasingly to be the sensible trace of the dissolution of the narrator's body, his desire to find and decipher her teeth, a desire to be found and deciphered himself. Poe's narrator begs our attentiveness to himself in his repeated assertions that "it is more than probable that [he is] not understood" (211). His wish to appropriate the teeth—"I coveted them so madly" (216)—is also a wish to be appropriated by them ("still the *phantasma* of the teeth maintained its terrible ascendancy"; 216). As Kaja Silverman has noted, "since we ourselves are always being photographed by [the gaze as Lacan defines it] even as we look, all binarizations of spectator and spectacle mystify the scopic relations in which we are held. The subject is generally both" ("Fassbinder and Lacan," 77). In the Kleinian sense in which part objects are often "won or lost by the subject . . . because he *is* those objects,"[15] the narrator of "Berenice" is alternately preserved and destroyed by the very teeth he so desperately wishes to preserve and to destroy.

*

A suggestive case of a different kind of confusion, another sort of production by the gaze of bodies and parts that seem literally separate from the viewer but figurally the same, is Hugo von Hofmannsthal's "Märchen der 672. Nacht" (1895). There are no teeth floating about in this tale, or severed hands, and yet the eyes and hands and faces of four servants become for the protagonist so much parts of himself, such examples of what he chooses to see, that in the end, like the teeth and in just as spectacular fashion, they fully succeed both in preserving his sense of himself and in leading him to his inevitable destruction.

He is a wealthy merchant's son intoxicated by the "profound" loveliness of his belongings. In these, he feels, are embodied all the shapes and colors of the world ("alle Formen und Farben der Welt").[16] In their company his days move more "beautifully" and "less emptily" (16). He counts among them his four servants, with whom after a time he is entirely preoccupied, and by whose features he becomes, little by little, haunted. He thinks about the white face and white hands of his housekeeper, whose voice recalls the voice of his mother; about the thin lips and pale eyebrows of the fifteen-year-old girl she takes in; about the somber, mulberry-hued face of his manservant; about the "lovely temples," the head, the eyelids, and lips of his young maid (20). These eyes and eyelids and eyebrows and hands and lips increasingly dominate his life until he feels so keenly the looks emanating from them, as he himself obsessively watches, that he is unable to think of anything else. Sitting in his garden, without so much as raising his head, he knows that "the eyes of the two girls [are] fixed upon him," that they are contemplating "his deepest being, his secret human inadequacy" (19).[17] When his manservant has ceased for a moment to look, has stepped away from the window, he knows this too, each time waiting "in secret fear" (19) for his return. And he knows when the old woman is sitting by her window watching, "her bloodless hands on the sun-drenched sill, the bloodless mask of her face an ever more terrible setting for her helpless black eyes, which could not die" (19).

On the one hand his servants torment him, "[circle] him like dogs" (16) with their incessant watching, are a "heavy weight" upon his limbs (19). Worst of all, they force him, he says, to think of himself "in a fruitless and . . . exhausting fashion" (19), so that, in the end, he can hardly move or think or feel except in the light of their presence. On the other hand, when he learns one day through an anonymous letter that he really ought to let one of his servants go, it seems to him as if someone were insulting and threatening the things most deeply his, as if they were trying to force him "to flee from himself" (21). He leaves his servants in order to answer the letter in town, but their parts and faces only circle about him there with greater frenzy. As he gazes into a silver mirror in a shop, he sees, in "another, inner mirror" (23), the image of the "[beautiful] head" of his maid. In a little child he confronts in a garden, who stares at him angrily through the glass panes, he sees the parts of the fifteen-year-old girl who had been brought in by the housekeeper: "Everything was the same, the pale eyebrows, the fine, trembling nostrils, the thin lips" (24–25). In the blossoms of some wax flowers he sees faces that he describes in a way that recalls the housekeeper: "In their rigidity [they] bore little resemblance to living flowers and were rather like masks, treacherous masks with their eye sockets grown shut" (26).

The circling and confusion of bodies and faces around him begin to generalize, to implicate increasingly his own body, and to turn his body into the body of a child. He stares at a narcissus, never feeling he had seen enough (24). He finds himself hanging desperately from an iron grating, helplessly, feeling as though his fingers were the fingers of a child. In the malicious, angry look of a horse he suddenly recalls the contorted face of an ugly poor man he had seen when he was very young, and with "childlike longing" throughout he thinks about "the beauty of his own wide bed" (27). At the end of the tale he will whimper like a child in his misery.

It is as though his own body had been threatening to be revealed all along in the bodies, faces, expressions, parts of his servants—as though the images he had been seeing (often in mirrors) should have been of himself from the very first. They become so now, the angry face of the child recalling in his mind the face of the fifteen-year-old girl, and then the angry child he himself once was. An ugly horse's face, similarly, recalls to him the poor man's face, then becomes a perfect image of what in the end will be his own contorted features. Just as the horse has "angry, rolling eyes, . . . curled-back nostrils, . . . [and] raised upper lips exposing the corner teeth of the upper jaws" (29), his own expression at the conclusion of the tale will be angry and alien (in his excruciating pain following the horse's kick to his groin), with his lips torn, and his teeth and gums laid bare.

For many fantastic narrators, and certainly for this merchant's son, the objects and bodies that appear to be points of obsession are already "lost objects"—objects that have assumed the value of, and are consequently felt to be, parts lost from the self. Lacan has called them "objets petit autre," suggesting they are constituted precisely as objects that are neither felt to be fully a part of the self nor sensed entirely as other. Kaja Silverman finds their perfect illustration in Orson Welles's film *Citizen Kane*, a film organized, she suggests, around the moment that ruptures simultaneously young Charles Kane's relationship with his mother and with his sled, named "Rosebud." "Rosebud" becomes, then, on the manifest level, "the most profound lost object," and through the remainder of the film Kane will be seen "obsessively collecting objects in a vain attempt to compensate for its loss, a loss which he experiences as an amputation" (*The Subject of Semiotics*, 157).

The merchant's son's preoccupations in "Das Märchen der 672. Nacht" fit a similar pattern, with the difference that his obsessive collecting is continually painful, continually verging on failure, and ends with what he interprets as his "collection's" betrayal of him. As he lies slowly dying in a desolate room, it is with the bitter feeling that his servants, whose parts had driven him from one part of the town to the next, had driven him in fact to his death (30). The text itself seems to want to make a pathetic point of this, for the distorted nightmare of bodily parts that the merchant's son suffers at the end contrasts sharply with his earlier happy dream of life, taking its own natural course toward death,

and of death "coming slowly up over the bridge, the bridge borne
on winged lions and leading to the palace" (16).

Yet the narrator isn't exempt, it seems to me, from the vision
that has been horrific; he has repeated his protagonist's vision and
entered into the horror that has led to the other's death. In this tale
where, unusually, the narrator and protagonist are not identical,
it is the narrator's report, the narrator's looking, that captures the
frightening features of the other's face in the final lines, where we
read: "Finally he vomited bile, then blood, and died with his features contorted, his lips so torn that his teeth and gums were laid
bare, giving him an alien, threatening expression" (30).

*

To fantasize aggression is to turn it round upon oneself: such
is the moment of autoeroticism, in which the indissoluble
bond between fantasy as such, sexuality, and the unconscious is confirmed.

—Jean Laplanche, *Life and Death in Psychoanalysis*

I have asked how we might understand the object viewed by
the fantastic protagonist, suggesting that it seems to function on
both the literal and the figurative planes, and as a body that is both
self and other. I have also suggested that "self" and "other" in
these texts seem to follow a rather distinct pattern, with self most
often signifying male (in these tales of invariably male protagonists), and other, with rare exceptions, signifying female. Poe's
"Tell-Tale Heart" is one of those exceptions (it is the eye and the
old man who are other to the narrator), while Hofmannsthal's
"Märchen der 672. Nacht" records a scattering of images from
several different male and female bodies to produce collectively
for the merchant's son an unwanted, distorted return to himself.
But most often—as in "Berenice," "Le Pied de momie," "Arria
Marcella," "La Chevelure," "Une heure ou la vision," "Der
Sandmann," "Le Chef-d'œuvre inconnu," "The Birthmark,"
"Gradiva," and *L'Eve future*—the body dismembered belongs to
a single female individual, and she or her part is typically silent—
indeed, often dead—erotically valued, and dangerous in some
positive or negative way.

In some sense fantastic discourse is a terrifying working out of all that is phallocentric. Whatever anguish is at stake, whatever material world is to be understood, whatever erotic value is to be culled from a viewing in parts, these are written again and again into the surface of a female body that is idealized, specularized, and gazed upon with all the loving abuse of the voyeur. Whether it is Maupassant's madman ecstatically enjoying the *chevelure*, or the narrator of "Berenice" cruelly extracting the teeth of his cousin, the female body is appropriated into the male, fetishized to reduce the agony of the lack it represents, left voiceless, when not visionless, in its dismembered form. Woman *is*, in these texts, as often as she is terrifying, a locus of possible delight. But in either case she is neither distinct nor individual, but a contrary, an opposite. In the terms of Josette Féral, she is the "instrument by which man attains unity, and she pays for it at the price of her own dispersion."[18]

The female body in these texts is the object of a gaze that in Western culture has itself been defined as a male affair, which tends already to invite a feminine form. "In a world ordered by sexual imbalance," Laura Mulvey has written, "pleasure in looking has been split between active/male and passive/female. . . . From pin-ups to striptease, from Ziegfeld to Busby Berkeley, [woman] holds the look, plays to and signifies male desire" ("Visual Pleasure and Narrative Cinema," 11). It is true that Mulvey collapses here, somewhat, the dynamic of male looking, in particular, with the gaze in general. But as Kaja Silverman notes, she does so because in Hollywood film "the male subject generally strives to disburden himself of lack, and the look is the most typical conduit of this disburdening. Within the classic cinematic text, woman, object of the male look, functions as the site at which male insufficiency is deposited, a projection which is preliminary to those defenses against castration anxiety [that Mulvey] theorize[s]" ("Fassbinder and Lacan," 59–60). Nor is reading *against* this look easily managed, and I refer now both to film and to fiction. Whether one identifies with the anxious male subject or with the dismembered (if occasionally empowered) object of that vision, one finds one's position (active or passive, male or female, anxious or horrified) ever threatening to collapse into the opposing one. That look, in the invitation to collaborate it extends to the reader, is not unlike the one realized in film, where reader is replaced by spectator and where audience participation is at the heart of the production of thrill. Thus "cinefantastic" horror, as Carol Clover has noted, turns on the equation "victim = audience,"[19] and succeeds in producing sensation "to more or less the degree that it succeeds in incorporating its spectators as 'feminine' and then violating that body—which recoils, shudders, cries out collectively—in ways otherwise imaginable, for males, only in nightmare" (213).

But fantastic narrative, I would suggest, also subverts the very condition of possibility of phallocentric discourse, underlining as it does the profound sense in which masculinity (indeed all subjectivity) is always disintegrating, always castrated, always an idealized and perilous construction. This narrative form reveals the wounds that that discourse, in order to work, is normally required to hide, "speaks" feminine mutilation in a language of transparently male agony, reminds the reader that, as Kaja Silverman notes, "there is ultimately no affirmation more central to our present symbolic order, yet . . . more precariously maintained, than the fiction that the exemplary male subject is adequate to the paternal function" ("Fassbinder and Lacan," 65). As the narrator of "Berenice" meditates in his library chamber, as the madman of "La Chevelure" raves in his insane asylum, as the narrator of "Gradiva" dreams, as Roderick Usher writes his excited poems, as the narrator of "Arria Marcella" recounts his baffling memories, the figure of woman is omnipresent and absent at the same time. She decenters fantastic discourse at the very moment her body provides central momentum. She splits it in two at the juncture of her own shattering. When she is appropriated, moreover, it is not without a trace, for her dismembered parts mar only too clearly what in other texts is often an apparently smooth and untroubled course. She becomes in the end so much the site of the displaced anguish of the protagonist himself in the face of his own falling apart, so often the name of his inability to give up the "past bliss" of (or retrospective desire for) wholeness and nonseparation, that the dismembering of her body is less significantly the dismembering of *her* body (though it is this fracturing that is, for us, most visible) than it is the severing, and contemplation in pieces, of the body of the protagonist.

One thinks of Nancy Vickers's suggestive essay, "Diana Described: Scattered Woman and Scattered Rhyme," where she sees Petrarch's rhymes to Laura (in his *Rime sparse*) as a striking example and origin of a tradition that views woman's beauty as a "composite of details" (97) and as a defense against male self-shattering. She traces this gesture back to the myth described in Ovid's *Metamorphoses* in which Actaeon's forbidden look at Diana leads the goddess to transform him into a helpless, voiceless stag, to be attacked and dismembered by his own hounds. Petrarch, then, is a "modern Actaeon," she suggests, unwilling to permit Ovid's angry goddess to speak her displeasure and deny his voice. He cannot allow Laura to dismember *his* body, and so, instead, "repeatedly, although reverently, scatters hers throughout his scattered rhymes" (109). And one thinks of Susan Gubar's suggestion that the female body is "feared for its power to articulate itself." She notes the woman's hair in Eliot's *Waste Land* that "glow[s] into words," and, in *The Great Gatsby*, "the 'black rivulets' of mascara on a weeping woman [that] lead to the 'humorous suggestion . . . that she sing the notes on her face' " (" 'The Blank Page' and the Issues of Female Creativity," 76).

Woman's dismembered body suggests, finally, the mother's body, and that body too is, or once was felt to be, one's own. Hence the merchant's son, in the tale by Hofmannsthal, collects what seem to be parts of himself dating back to a time when they belonged to some other's (perhaps the mother's) body—to a time when that other was also himself. In Maupassant's "La Chevelure," similarly, the madman insists, "It seemed to me that I had already lived before, that I must have known this woman" (111), as though he recognized in the mesh of hair (and in the body it represents) both something he knew before, and something he knew as part of himself. He follows these words with a sudden reciting of two stanzas from the famous medieval poem, "Ballade des dames du temps jadis" (The ballad of women of times past), a poem that is itself a suggestion of some lost, feminine ordering of things. Villon's poem is a detailed calling up of women from the past and, in a sense, of images of the mother's breast. Its refrain—"But where are the snows of last winter?"[20]—sings of earlier whiteness.

In analogous fashion, as the narrator in "Berenice" recollects "past bliss," he also confuses memories of himself with what would seem to be memories of his mother. His assertion, "it is mere idleness to say that I had not lived before," curiously takes as its evidence of truth his "remembrance of aerial forms—of spiritual and meaning eyes—of sounds, musical yet sad; a remembrance which will not be excluded" (209–10). If I have read this tale as a story about loss—loss of harmony, of rainbows, of youth, of meaning, of wholeness, and of the mother—and about the nostalgic desire to return to these, the narrator's return to Berenice's tomb at the end of the tale, and Berenice's own "return" to life, become the marks of a kind of revitalized pathway of exchange, mother to son, that the narrator has been trying to restore, in his perverse way, from the very beginning.

The body in pieces in fantastic narrative would seem inadequately described in *any* reading that reads too singly its various contours. In my discussion of a gaze that is a multiple and layered vision, in my suggestion that metaphor and metonymy, Symbolic and Imaginary, are all terms that throw light on a complex, visual/textual web of movement and of blockage, I have tried to show that we cannot ever, fully and finally, name the object viewed by the fantastic protagonist, nor yet understand perfectly the position from which it is seen. It is only partly true to say that that body is a reflection of woman as icon, or that it represents some recollected maternal plenitude, or, indeed, that in Poe's "The Tell-Tale Heart" it is *not* a feminine body. I would suggest, rather, that fantastic narrative gains its greatest power from its ability to recount, despite itself, the truth of its own failure. When its parts don't come together, don't succeed in reducing the agony that produces them, don't cover up the confusion of bodies from which they are generated (as they might in a more nearly "perfect" phallocentric discourse), the tale itself succeeds in displaying its seduction by the body that isn't simply feminine, isn't simply the mother, isn't simply, and only, an other's body. Its meaning, instead, oscillates between the literal one figured by the text's and by the subject's look, and the figural one, which is disfigured by those same agents.

Philippe Sollers has written, as I cite at the opening of my introduction, that the body is "that tapestry in which our form shifts and changes . . . ; it is the 'continuous' from which we fashion, for ourselves and for others, a visible discontinuity that demands its due" ("Le Toit: essai de lecture systématique," 179). In these words, as in the texts we have considered, the "shifting form" is certainly our own form (or that of the protagonist), and it is also the only continuity we ever have. Simultaneously, however, it is a "tapestry," a visible witness to discontinuity, a body that is in fact, also and always, an other's body. Hence these narrators' ultimate fascination, and ours when we share in their look: their pleasure, mixed with horror, in contemplating its separate pieces.

CHAPTER 4

The Body of Madness

If it is true . . . that the question underlying madness *cannot be asked*, that language is not *capable* of asking it . . . , it is . . . not less true that, in the fabric of a text, . . . the question is *at work*, stirring, changing place, and wandering away.

—Shoshana Felman, "Madness and Philosophy *or* Literature's Reason"

I suggested in Chapters 1 and 2 that the body in pieces in fantastic narrative appears at times an eerie product of language, at others an object that squarely resides within the tangible world of the text. Clearly, it is a body that is an extraordinary, often baffling blend of significations. In the fragile space of the narrator's or protagonist's gaze, it becomes a body in which the tangible and the figural meet, each of these dimensions adding to while also undermining fundamentally the weight and outline of the other. These texts and the images within them refuse all possible enclosure of meaning, undermine every category of ontological stability. They place in jeopardy every normal division between what is subject and what is object, between what is inside the body and what outside. The precarious balance that results, the balance between some viewing narrator or protagonist and the fragmented body that is encountered, functions best at the moment it is ready to collapse—at that point where the subject's own body voyeuristically overlaps with the body it erotically engages, where its gaze falters between the rigid vision of the adult and the more fluid vision of the child, where its aggression, so often

against the feminine, becomes (or shows itself to be) a perfect aggression against its self.

Here there is not the normal "mastery" of the text over its image content, what Fredric Jameson has seen to be the literary text's usual "sedimenting" of signification, its usual transformation of an always latent Imaginary into the Symbolic. There is, instead, as I have tried to show, a reversal of this process and a continual movement toward radical blurring. From within the Symbolic realm of the text emerges the outline of an otherwise lost Imaginary, while the protagonist would seem to wish to catapult the body in pieces out of language entirely—out of memory, out of imagination and all play of imagoes, into some place of pure sensation (into the "real"?) where it might survive, intact, the valorizing or critical judgment of reader, listener, spectator, or self.

In this nonplace, in this slippery excess where more tangible and more figural significations collide, the fragmented body reveals its affinities with the dynamics of madness, with even its "shape." For madness too, like the body in pieces in fantastic narrative, resists mastery, resists the Symbolic, resists all interpretation. An "active incompletion of a meaning that ceaselessly transforms itself, offers itself but to be misunderstood, misapprehended,"[1] madness seems to be a condition of otherness inside the self, a reading of a mind out of sync with the body it inhabits, a state of division where the hand might flutter uncontrollably because in fact it belongs to "someone else" or to "another me," where the lips might move but utter sentences incomprehensible to the speaker.[2] Madness has a way of exploding every possible unity, whether on the level of the world, of language, or of reason. Like the body in these tales, it operates from within and further produces a kind of rhetoric of the fragment, rhetoric that both incites and makes impossible every effort at achieving wholeness.

For all these reasons madness and the fragmented body in these tales often appear allied. In "Berenice" the narrator's concern with his cousin's teeth and the increasing dissolution of her body are framed within his avowal of a "morbid" disease. In "The Fall of the House of Usher" the splitting apart of Roderick's psyche is equally experienced as the fracturing of his sister's body and as the falling apart of the house they inhabit. In Hoffmann's "Der Sandmann" those moments that could be read as moments of hysterical illusion are marked by legs twisted in their sockets, by eyes yanked out, by eyeglasses winking and blinking. One begins to wonder whether it is madness, with its disjointed visions, that produces the body in pieces in these tales, or whether instead those very fragments (fragments that fail in the end to relieve the anxiety lying behind them) produce the madness. Or is it possible, as I will suggest, that madness and the body are not at all causally linked, *not* productive of each other, but rather terms that productively (and much more interestingly) intersect?

To conclude that the fragments dispersed throughout these texts themselves provoke the madness is, I think, to overprivilege the tangible dimensions of the body in pieces and to underprivilege its production within a particular gaze. It is to suggest that the old man's "vulture eye," in Poe's "The Tell-Tale Heart," *is*, and this too simply, an eye that unduly offends, emitting a light so perfectly hellish that it drives the narrator to excessive violence; that, in Hoffmann's "Der Sandmann," the gruesome parts of Coppelius, remembered so vividly by Nathanael from a childhood during which he was tormented by them, are the root of Nathanael's later development; that a father's rebellious hand, in Maupassant's "Le Tic" (1884), may be traced entirely to the sight of the severed finger of the daughter he had just entombed.

To conclude, on the other hand, that it is madness that produces the body in pieces is to say, just as unsatisfactorily, that this body is merely the figural product of a diseased and imaginative subjectivity, and a body that may be dismissed. This would seem to be the position of Tzvetan Todorov, whose *Introduction à la littérature fantastique* remains, as I have noted, the best-known and most influential treatment of the genre. For Todorov madness is a natural pathology, and when we are sure it is present (as from the testimony of an "objective" narrator), all strangeness in a given story becomes fully explainable by it. The reader, according to Todorov, need no longer "hesitate" in interpreting story

events—need no longer feel, in this context, that there *is* a literal
piece—need no longer feel ambivalent whether to read these texts
in a natural or in a supernatural way. (With the loss of such necessary hesitation, indeed, these texts, according to Todorov, no
longer belong to the fantastic as a genre. He suggests that only
when we are unsure whether madness is present or not, and
strictly in this uncertainty, is the genre once again possible.)

From either of these two perspectives textual richness is
blocked; in either case madness and the body in pieces each become a tool with which to glance past the other. In the first instance madness is all too easily explained with the privileging of
the "literal" bodily piece, while in the second, though Todorov
wasn't speaking of the body in pieces when he conceived his theory, that broken-up body—from Berenice's teeth to the coveted
mesh of hair in Maupassant's "La Chevelure"—becomes either
suspect or laughable. It finds itself excluded *along with* madness,
becomes, like madness, a term we needn't read further. When Todorov insists, moreover, that the reader's "hesitation" in interpreting story events cannot take place when madness is present to
"explain" the nature of a text's images, he not only elides the difficulties posed by the first-person narrative but also repeats a distinctly Cartesian, tautological illogic. He insists that our interpretive judgment is necessarily reasonable—that our interpretive
reason is exempt from the hesitations madness itself might provoke, just as the Cartesian subject (in *Les Méditations*) feels its reason automatically exempt from "the black vapors" of the insane.
In his first meditation Descartes reassures his reader that of some
things he is absolutely sure, if for no other reason than that otherwise he would have to compare himself to those madmen "whose
brains are so disturbed":

> And how could I deny that these hands and this body are mine? un-
> less perhaps I were to compare myself to those madmen whose
> brains are so disturbed . . . by the black vapors of the bile that they
> insist they are kings while they are very poor; that they are clothed
> in gold and purple while they are completely naked; or imagine
> themselves to be jugs or to have a body of glass.[3]

It would seem not only that madness for Descartes is best expressible through the dismembered body, a body he will then try to put back together, but also that the subject of *Les Méditations* too easily makes an end of the problem of interpretation, "hides within its use of the first person," as Dalia Judovitz has noted, "its complicity with language, fiction, and representation" (*Subjectivity and Representation in Descartes*, 139). Despite its reliance on the baroque themes of dreams, waking, and madness, the Cartesian subject "constitute[s] itself as precluding them" (5). It constructs "the fiction of a philosophical system that is in fact free of all deception," and proves eventually that it is not asleep, not deluded, not mad, because it says so.[4] One thinks of the narrator of Poe's "The Black Cat" (1843) who with similar conviction insists: "Mad indeed would I be to expect [belief], in a case where my very senses reject their own evidence. Yet, mad am I not—and very surely do I not dream."[5]

Having insisted, finally, that it "knows" its own ("madly" dismembered) body because, precisely, it is not mad, the Cartesian subject also insists that it is only reasonable to the degree it is able to forget that body—to the extent it is willing *not* to know it. It unites the "unreason" it finds improper in the thinking subject to a corporeality whose false sensations are implicated in that unreason. It explains that the very body that proves its reason offers to its judgment erroneous data:

> I will shut my eyes, now, I will stop up my ears, I will turn away all my senses, even erase from my thoughts all images of corporeal things, or, at very least, because this can hardly be done, I will consider them to be vain and false; and in this way, engaging in conversation only my self, and contemplating my interior, I shall strive to make me, little by little, better known to myself. (*Méditations*, 284)

Not every critic, of course, has read Descartes's *Méditations* in this way. Michel Foucault, Francis Barker, and Dalia Judovitz are skeptical of the Cartesian subject. In their respective works (*Histoire de la folie à l'âge classique; The Tremulous Private Body: Es-*

says on Subjection; and *Subjectivity and Representation in Descartes: The Origins of Modernity*) they have pointed especially to the way in which Descartes's subject naively dismisses, one by one, all the forms of illusion "in the *doubling* of a consciousness that never separates from itself, and does not *split*" (Foucault, *Histoire de la folie*, 48). Jacques Derrida, however, provides a different view. In reply to Foucault he proposes (in his essay "Cogito et histoire de la folie") that the exclusion of madness in Descartes's first meditation is meant ironically. The Cartesian project, he feels, recognizes in madness its very freedom and possibility, "only pretends to exclude it in the first phase of its first argument" ("Cogito," 87). In rebuttal to this Foucault insists that Derrida misreads Descartes for his own strong purposes. In his words: "One needs perhaps to ask oneself how an author as meticulous as Derrida . . . was able not only to commit so many omissions, but also to manufacture so many displacements, so many inversions, so many substitutions?" ("La Folie, l'absence d'œuvre," 602). It is Foucault's opinion (and he argues persuasively) that Derrida flattens and in the end dismisses the Cartesian exclusion of madness in order to keep madness for philosophy: in order that "the possibility be excluded, finally, that philosophical discourse exclude madness."[6]

My own reading of Descartes resonates most closely with those of Foucault, Barker, and Judovitz, who see Descartes's exclusion of madness as a blindness to the ironies of madness itself, and as a blindness that undermines his argument fundamentally. And I see Todorov's expelling of madness from the domain of the "true" fantastic as a move that betrays a similarly flawed logic. Todorov doesn't ask what is going on inside the madness in so many tales, or what its presence might signify, but merely, and too simply, whether madness is present or not. While he may be right in finding central to the genre the "hesitation" a reader experiences in interpreting the text, his own too brittle categories— of natural versus supernatural, of reason versus madness, and of madness, it seems to me, disallowed its own inscrutability—undo the richness this concept brings. If the Cartesian subject, in some

critics' view, proves that he is not mad because he says so, Todorov fixes the limits of a genre according to an interpretive response that is invulnerable to the most profound hesitations this
genre may seek to elicit.

If there is no understanding madness; if it "cannot be said"
(Derrida, "Cogito et histoire de la folie," 60) but can only be
misapprehended, misunderstood (Foucault, "La Folie, l'absence
d'œuvre"); if we are "unable to locate it, read it, except where it
already has escaped" (Felman, "Madness and Philosophy," 228),
then certainly there is no dismissing it—no Todorovian expelling
from the fantastic all those texts where madness is clearly at stake,
any more than one may expel madness from the domain of reason. Madness and reason are too inextricably linked, are each, as
Shoshana Felman puts it, "*an act of faith* in reason." Indeed, if
what characterizes madness is "a blindness *blind to itself*, to the
point of necessarily entailing an *illusion of reason* . . . no reasonable conviction can . . . be exempt from the suspicion of madness" (Felman, "Madness and Philosophy," 206).

*

I would like to propose in this chapter that the body in pieces
and madness—but madness in all its complexity and in its intimate, often paradoxical alignment with reason—be viewed in
fantastic narrative not in any causal relation but rather as parallel
processes: as processes that intersect and that become, consequently, doubly disturbing. I would suggest that they are allied
as two related signifiers might be for a signified that remains elusive, each one expressing, reading, measuring the other in the absence of some third, more meaningful term. Overlapping at
times but still distinct, they would have a similar but separate
stake in the crumbling house of "The Fall of the House of
Usher," in the dissolution of Berenice, in the emergence of the
tiny foot of *La Belle-Noiseuse*, in the rebelliousness of an aging
father's hand in Maupassant's "Le Tic," where "each time he
wished to grasp an object, his hand made a sudden swerve, a kind
of mad zigzag, before settling finally on the thing it was reaching
for."[7] Each would find its energies doubled in Maupassant's "Le

Horla" in the production of a veritable "body" of madness that
gradually takes over the narrator, drinking his milk, crushing his
chest, inhaling his reason as it sucks at his mouth, covering his
reflection as he glances in the direction of a mirror. Far from providing for us each other's "answer," madness and the fragmented
body in these texts would equally hide, or falsely name, an otherwise inaccessible question.

To analyze closely Maupassant's "Qui sait?" ("Who Knows?"
1890) is to see more precisely how the above proposition might
work. For here madness provides the perfect stage for the body
in pieces—in this case, for a house (a body) full of errant furniture—while the body in pieces stands in synecdochically, so to
speak, for the narrator's possible "madness." Yet neither measures alone the way in which this text is never stable, never completely significant in the way we expect it to be. At best they point
together to a blurring of boundaries that separately makes each
one possible—to a confusion of inside and outside that motivates
both the fragments that litter the text and the madness that serves
to frame them.

The narrator is a man who has always lived alone. He is "a
solitary man, a dreamer, a sort of isolated philosopher" for whom
the presence of others incites intolerable distress.[8] In Paris he is in
infinite agony; he cannot tolerate "that immense crowd that
swarms, [and] that surrounds me even when it is sleeping"
(1226). At home he cannot sleep when he senses the sleep of others nearby: "I can never sleep when I know, when I sense, behind
a wall, existences interrupted by . . . regular eclipses of reason"
(1226). He rarely leaves his home, has grown attached to its every
inanimate object, has adorned it little by little with chairs and sofas and favorite knickknacks "as reassuring to my eyes as faces"
(1226). His house, with all its separate objects, can be seen as functioning as the whole and the parts of a body to which he is both
erotically and narcissistically attached. He speaks of his "tenderness" (1232) for the objects around him and of their reassuring
familiarity. He tells how he has so filled and "dressed" his house
that he is as happy in it as though clasped in the arms of a woman

whose cherished embrace has become "a calm, sweet need" (1226). His house is both a refuge from and erotic replacement for the bodies of others and, as I will show in a moment, a body charged narcissistically as his own.

One can imagine then his horror on seeing, one night, on returning home from the opera, the exodus from his house of every piece of his furniture—on hearing the tumultuous sound of a marching on his stairs and then seeing his great easy chair leaving "with a waddling gait [*en se dandinant*]" (1229), his low settees dragging themselves along like crocodiles, his footstools trotting away like rabbits:

> Oh! what emotion!. . . . My piano, my grand piano, galloped by with the speed of a frenzied horse and with a murmur of music in its flank; the smallest objects slid along the sand like ants. . . . I saw my desk appear. . . .
> Suddenly I was no longer afraid, I threw myself onto it and I seized it the way one seizes a thief, the way one seizes a woman who flees; but it continued its irresistible course. (1229–30)

The extraordinary event would seem at first to narrate the nightmarish effect of a madman's delusions. Or, if the narrator is not mad, this event would appear instead to represent (and this is Todorov's view) something utterly "fantastic," something that intrudes without warning, simply and inexplicably, and that disappears only to return with all its power just prior to the end of the tale. In Todorov's words, "There is no logic in the behavior of the furniture," there are "no preparations for the fantastic before its abrupt intrusion" (104, 88).

Yet in my view, the complex threads that link the event's description both to the passages that precede it and to the ones that follow indicate a blurring of ontological boundaries so textually and linguistically rich that to call it madness and leave it at that is to radically abbreviate one's reading, while to throw up one's hands at the event's "simple" strangeness is to sever its crucial ties to the larger tale, to miss an instability operating at every level that is both inexplicable and full of meaning.[9] If one could say, for example, that there is a question here of the limits and the possible reversals imaginable between the animate and the inanimate, such reversals are already subtly at stake in the opening passages. There, solitude takes place in the midst of objects that are as familiar as human faces, the crowd remains a crowd even when it is sleeping, while sleep provokes such regular "eclipses of reason" that it renders its subjects, in a sense, inanimate. Oppositions of every nature continue to dominate these early passages as waking life is opposed to sleep, as solitary sleep is played against sleep that is restless, while those people who need the company of others are set against those who don't. The ones, the narrator says, "are gifted for living outside themselves, the others for living inside" (1226). Madness itself is opposed to reason in the very lines with which the narrator begins his story, when, with strikingly Cartesian certainty, he asserts:

> If I were not sure of what I saw—sure that there was not, in my reasoning, a single weakness, a single error in my judgment, a single gap in the inflexible steps of my observations, I would believe myself a simple madman, the plaything of a strange vision. After all, who knows? (1225)

The difference between this narrator and Descartes, of course, lies in that final line, in the question, "After all, who knows?" Unlike the subject of *Les Méditations*, a subject equally involved in self-narration and who in similar fashion functions simultaneously "as author and actor, spectator and play" (Judovitz, 138), *this* narrator steps back to qualify his certainty; he places a question mark between the "inflexible steps" of his observations and the possibility of some "strange vision." Every opposition to follow will be a revision of the narrator's opening words—a setting at odds, a playing against, a running together of terms that belong now to logic, now to language, now to metaphorization, now to the world—a blurring that dares us to put it aside or to call it names, but that is all the more tantalizing the more closely we read it.

In this light the exodus of the narrator's furniture becomes a kind of violent climax to the text's general and pervasive shifting of terms: it represents a more radical version of objects "familiar . . . as human faces," of crowds that swarm "even when [they are] sleeping." Indeed, if the narrator's house and all its separate objects, as I have suggested, are seen to function as the whole and the parts of a body to which the narrator is both erotically and narcissistically attached, then in retrospect those ontological jeopardies that are present earlier in the text acquire clearer meaning: in this case the sleep of others nearby would irritate for its transgression of the narrator's own physical limits; familiar knickknacks would be reassuring for their equation with the parts of the narrator's own body; sleep itself would become the "lifeless" state that would describe the stillness both of objects and of persons.

The narrator's double relation to his house *as* body, finally, allows for yet further doublings of meaning. I have noted that it is a relation of self to other. It is not surprising, then, that the objects that seduce and betray him are gendered feminine. That very gendering both keeps them at a distance and makes them more readily subject to aggressive desire. I have also suggested that this relation is one of self to self, a narcissistic refinding of his insides elsewhere. Hence the desk that he leaps upon ("the way one seizes a woman") contains, like his own body, "the whole history of my heart" (1230). As for his furniture, he approaches this later in the tale "tremblant de tous mes membres" (1233): trembling—the phrase can be read in both ways—both "in" and "from" (at the sight of) all the parts of his body. The exodus of his furniture will indeed represent, as he will tell us, "a formidable tumult" (1229). But it is a tumult that repeats and brings to a climax (one could almost say an onanistic one) an uproar that begins internally. In the following passage, situated in the text just prior to the extraordinary exodus, which I quote at length for all its richness, we are able to see the way in which the interior of the narrator's body blends almost imperceptibly with the interior of his house: we observe as certain "tressaillements" (quiverings) felt in the skin, certain "ronflements" (rumblings) sensed in the ears are exchanged for a sound heard "à travers" (through) the wall, that becomes, in the end, "un grondement d'impatience, de colère, d'émeute mystérieuse" (a roar of impatience, of anger, of mysterious riot). It captures what the narrator felt that night, approaching his house in the darkness, feeling that the trees surrounding it were like a tomb "in which [his] house was buried" (1227).

> With each advancing step I felt quiverings in my skin, and once in front of the wall of my vast dwelling . . . I sensed that I would have to wait a few moments before opening the door and entering. I . . . sat down on a bench, below the windows of my drawing room. I remained there slightly vibrating, my head leaning against the high wall, my eyes opened onto the shadows of the foliage. During these initial moments I noticed nothing unusual about me. There was some rumbling in my ears; but this often happens to me. It seems to me, at times, that I hear trains passing, that I hear bells ringing, that I hear a crowd marching.
>
> Soon, however, these rumblings became more distinct, more precise, more recognizable. I had been mistaken. It wasn't the usual whirring of my arteries that had put this clamour in my ears, but a noise that was very specific, though very indistinct, that was coming, without a doubt, from the interior of my house.
>
> I could distinguish it through the wall, this continuous noise, rather an agitation than a noise, a vague stirring of a myriad of things as though someone were jostling, moving around, carefully dragging about all my furniture. . . .
>
> I waited for a long time unable to decide what to do, my mind lucid but madly anxious. I waited, standing there, still listening to this sound that kept on growing, . . . that seemed to become a roar of impatience, of anger, of mysterious riot.
>
> Then, suddenly, ashamed of my cowardice, I seized my keys, I chose the one that I needed, I thrust it into the lock, I turned it twice and, pushing with all my force I sent the door crashing against the wall.
>
> The blow rang out like a shot from a gun, and then, in reply to this sound of explosion, from the top to the bottom of my dwelling there was a formidable tumult. It was so sudden, so terrible, so deafening that I stepped back several paces and, though still feeling this was useless, drew from its holster my revolver. (1228–29)

The phrase with which the passage begins—"with each advancing step" (à mesure que j'avançais)—announces perfectly the account to follow, an account remembered as if incrementally. With a rhythm that is almost hypnotic the narrator advances toward, sits beside, then leans against the wall of his house while we are moved across the parts of his body, passing from his quivering skin to his vibrating head to his open eyes to his rumbling ears. We move, indeed, from the knowledge of the narrator's own internal sounds—the way he often seems to hear the passing of trains, the ringing of bells, the marching of crowds—to the image of a head as it leans "against the wall," hearing sounds that could just as easily be coming from *his* side of the wall as from the other.

The ambiguity of this exchange is cemented in the paragraphs that follow when the rumblings the narrator had sensed in his ears become a noise heard "through" (à travers) that wall. What might have been the usual "whirring" of his arteries, a sound that in fact he knows quite well, is coming, he says, from inside his house. We watch as "rumblings" become "a specific noise," as this "specific noise" becomes "an agitation," and as "agitation" increases to "a roar of impatience." When "mysterious riot" is physically launched with the narrator's opening the door of his house, it is as though the deafening tumult he hears had originated in the very quivering of his skin, in the very "whirring" of his arteries. Indeed, with its rhythmic buildup and explosive conclusion, it is as though the exchange that occurs had generated not just a melding of his body *with* his house, but also a sexually violent experience of that melding: when he finally opens the door he does so by seizing his key, thrusting it into the lock, turning it twice, and then pushing with all his force.

This exchange occurs, moreover, not just within the perfection of an image where meaning is ambiguous, where sounds are generated both from within and without, producing a noise that is both specific and indistinct. It occurs as well in the sonorities and subtleties of the language with which each image is constructed. Thus the narrator sits beside his house with open eyes, but with eyes opened onto a darkness (his eyes were opened onto "the shadows of the foliage"). He speaks of his house as his vast "dwelling" (*demeure*), a word that could in fact refer to his body, and then shifts to the word "house" (*maison*) the moment we move through the wall. He describes the sound he hears as "a formidable tumult," where "tumult" could be read either as "uproar" or as "confusion." And he describes this sound in a way that resonates with senses other than hearing, insisting, "I could *distinguish* it through the wall" (emphasis mine). Indeed, when what he hears finally becomes "deafening," the sound that had so far been at issue is replaced by a sound that obliterates the very possibility of hearing. The narrator is literally "exploded" into a scene that is not just audible but visual as well, one that leaves him wondering strangely whether to leave the scene or draw his gun. The emotion he feels, he tells us, is balanced precariously between clear thinking and mad anxiety.

Throughout this passage sound and scene remain as intimately bound as ever to earlier images and earlier moments. The exodus of the narrator's furniture is an event that, far from intruding into the text, reflects the details of its production from within the text. Thus, if the narrator had begun his account with the agony he feels in the midst of the crowds of Paris, and if we learn in the passage above the way in which he often hears in his head "marcher une foule" (a crowd marching), he will now, appropriately, be terrified by an endless "procession of furniture," an extraordinary "trampling" on "les marches" (the steps) of his staircase (1229). If before he had felt the crowds of Paris as a kind of death whose pain was registered in his physical being ("I die on some moral level, and am tortured as well in my body and in my nerves by this immense crowd that swarms"; 1226), the march of his furniture will be, literally, a murderous wounding of his legs and body, as it walks upon his limbs, "trampling" and "bruising them" (*les meurtrissant*; 1230). If earlier he had leaned against the wall of his house "slightly vibrating" (1228), he will now be faced with a sound of crutches of wood and of crutches of iron that were "vibrating" like cymbals (1229). When, finally,

his furniture has all departed, from the leaping chairs to the gal-
loping piano, he will flee to a hotel and wait, and listen to the
"leaping" of his heart (1230).

The narrator will in fact find these objects again in an antique
shop in Rouen that is, appropriately, another house, a "maison de
brocanteur" that he will also call a "cemetery for old furniture"
(1232–33). And, interestingly, they will be in the possession of a
man who, "very short and very fat, fat like a phenomenon, a hideous phenomenon" (1234) seems to be more object than any of
them:

> He had a sparse beard, with unequal, scattered, and yellowish hairs,
> and he hadn't a single hair on his head! Not a single hair? . . . His
> cranium appeared to me like a little moon in this huge room. . . .
> His face was lined and bloated, his eyes imperceptible. (1234)

As for the body that is the narrator's house, it will return to itself
at the end of the tale when the furniture returns, this time from
Rouen, while the narrator will flee to an asylum—to a house
([*une*] *maison de santé*; 1237) that he hopes will be a safer one.

Meantime, as if to enumerate the loss of his own body parts,
the narrator regrets "the most insignificant objects, the . . . most
modest, the least noticed that had ever belonged to me" (1230).
Simultaneously, and as if to regret the loss of an other's body—
the one in which he had felt as happy as though clasped in the arms
of a woman and that he had violated with the thrusting of his key
into its lock—he listens mournfully as the door of his house slams
shut, the one "that he himself had opened, enraged" (1230).

*

> We are talking about a figure that both secures and suspends
> meaning, manages an empty space where is only proposed
> the possibility—as yet unrealized—that a certain meaning
> will soon inhabit this space, or some other, or yet a third,
> and this, perhaps, to infinity.
> —Michel Foucault, "La Folie, l'absence d'œuvre"

The difficulty in reading such texts as Maupassant's "Qui
sait?"—in "reading" its body in pieces and in reading what could

be (but isn't necessarily) the narrator's madness—is the desire we feel, just like the narrator of this tale, to master unmasterable terms. As Christine Brooke-Rose has noted in a discussion of Clément Rosset's *Le Réel—traité de l'idiotie*, what makes reality most "tip over into nonsense is precisely the necessity we impose on it of always being significant."[10] To the degree that madness is, for the modern Western reasoning subject, a pathological and impossible *maladie* from which we must remain unquestionably separate, it also represents a language we are unused to hearing, a language strangely banished from the domain of language:

> Everything that characterizes the *spoken* world is prohibited to un-reason; madness is that language that is banished—the one that, against the code of language, enunciates words without meaning (the "insane," the "half-witted" . . .) or . . . words that are sac-rilegious (the violent, the furious) or yet the one that allows pro-hibited meanings. (Foucault, "La Folie," 579)

The problem of reading madness appears increasingly to be an extreme version of the problem of reading literature itself—of allowing a text its own, self-referential meaning. Foucault speaks of "that strange proximity between madness and literature," not-ing that literature, certainly since Mallarmé, presumes, "behind each of its sentences, behind each one of its words, the power to modify at will the values and the meanings of the language to which, despite all (and in fact it) it belongs" ("La Folie," 580). And, as my argument might suggest, the problem of reading madness would seem to be similar to the one of reading the body, that to-pos that is similarly double, similarly inaccessible, similarly (as Foucault points out) "a figure that both secures and suspends meaning" ("La Folie," 580). The body has been equally excluded, moreover, from modern constructions of subjectivity, as one sees so vividly in such texts as Descartes's *Méditations*. Hence the study of Francis Barker, who shows the way in which the body emerges from the seventeenth century (from the abstracting gaze of sci-ence and philosophy, and of the art that is a reflection of these) as an object that had "ceased to mean in any but residual ways" (*The*

Tremulous Private Body, 78). Relying on the work of Foucault, Barker traces the body's history from its spectacular presence on the Jacobean stage (where it was "judicially tortured" in the name of the king or "disassembled lovingly . . . in the cause of poetry"; 23) to its only slightly later place in the Shakespearean world where it was asked, more subtly, to fade from view.[11] Here Hamlet asks that this "too too solid flesh would melt, / Thaw and resolve itself into a dew!" (1.2.129–30). From such moments as these the seventeenth century, Barker suggests, determinedly takes its cue: in Samuel Pepys's *Diary* (written between 1660 and 1669) the body is "no more than a monstrous, residual irrationality which has had to be expelled from discourse" (66); in the *Méditations* (1641) the Cartesian subject is "radically undermined by the loss of . . . [a body] whose insistent reminders . . . it must ever attempt to quell" (60); and in Rembrandt's *Anatomy Lesson of Dr. Tulp* (1632; reproduced below), a portrait in which a group of surgeons dissects the arm of a corpse, despite the tantalizing flesh before them the surgeons' gazes are organized "in order not to see it" (77). They look either toward us or toward the anatomy book open at the foot of the corpse, making the body before them, as Barker points out, all but invisible.

The material body that had been, before the seventeenth century, a critical site for punishment is replaced in these texts by a body set aside as supplementary (to borrow a term from Derrida), a body "de-realized in thought" that nevertheless continued to provoke the most desperate gestures of domination. This was a body, furthermore, susceptible to radical division, unlike the mind (or soul), which was seen as one. As Descartes would write:

> The body, by its very nature, is always divisible. . . . And while the mind as a whole seems to be united to the body as a whole, still, if a foot, or an arm, or some other part is separated from my body, it is certain that, for this, nothing will be taken away from my mind. (*Méditations*, 330–31)

The body as we see it in seventeenth-century art and literature is a body that is more "modern" than ever before, as it is increas-

Fig. 4.2 Rembrandt van Rijn, *The Anatomy Lesson of Dr. Tulp* (Mauritshuis–The Hague; reproduced by permission)

ingly constructed by those powers of thought and imagination
that apprehend it. And yet, ironically, it is a body emphatically
outside language—"confined, ignored, excribed from discourse"
(Barker, 63). This century's creative imagination, Barker suggests, strove increasingly to confirm a "powering and powered
division between body and soul, object and subject, which
[would be] the principle of its sexuality, its epistemology and its
representation" (95).

*

In fantastic narrative, however, as in "Qui sait?" both madness and the body (the physical one) return—madness and its
"banished language" and the body that, in the seventeenth century, had been reduced to the "private residuality that haunts the
discourse of the subject" (Barker, 103). Though often in an un-
invited way, the body, as the nineteenth-century imagination
would construct it, steps up physically (perversely) onto center
stage. We find it mastering as much as mastered, subject as much
as object, masculine even where apparently feminine, where
"feminine" is another practical locus of mastery. (As I discuss in
Chapter 3, the partial body that seems so feminine often reflects
as well the shattered body of the [masculine] narrator himself.)
As for madness, it is given a voice. Foucault describes the almost
"lyrical" recognition of madness in the nineteenth century, while
Tobin Siebers notes that the Romantics, "disdainful of the exclusionary practices of the Enlightenment," struggled "not to exclude anything" (*The Romantic Fantastic*, 28). But the nineteenth
century's reembracing of madness was full of contradictions.
Hence Foucault's qualification: "This recognition, reflection, in
contradistinction to lyrical feeling, doesn't in any way accommodate. It protects itself from any such recognition, affirming
with an insistence that grows with time that the madman is nothing but an object, a medical object" (*Histoire de la folie*, 538).

   If madness is given a voice, moreover, it is one that doesn't,
for this, necessarily "speak" its meaning. It is a madness over
which we still must "hesitate," a madness that doesn't function
thematically, a madness that is a relation to discourse much more
than an object within it, ensuring *against* our understanding a tale

unless, perhaps, in the moment it slips away. Thus the difficulty in such schemes as Todorov's, where madness is viewed simply as "present or not," and if clearly present then a reason to "know" (to dismiss) certain of the meanings in a given text.[12] For Todorov madness is a pathological state that nullifies our interpretive hesitations and, in this, nullifies the fantastic; it is not, as it is for me, the element that renders this unstable form all the more interestingly unstable. When the narrator of Poe's "Tell-Tale Heart" plaintively asks, "Why *will* you say that I am mad? The disease had sharpened my senses—not destroyed—not dulled them" (792), it is surely from the feeling that neither he nor the reader is in a position to "say" what he is, to say what he "has," to say "madness," if it is madness.

However true it is, finally, that in the history of modern Western discourse madness and the body are excluded from language, it is here in fact that they find their best ally. Derrida has suggested that on the one hand the very nature of language—its "essential economy"—is to "break" with madness, explaining that "the sentence is by its very nature normal. It bears normality within itself, that is to say, *sense*, in every sense of the word" ("Cogito," 83–84). Yet he insists, on the other hand, that there is a "language" of fiction, or a "fiction" of language, that constitutes the only place in which madness can in fact be evoked: "Any speaking subject . . . having to evoke that madness that is at the heart of thought . . . can do so only in the dimension of *possibility* and in the language of fiction or in the fiction of language" ("Cogito," 84). Something occurs, it seems, within language's gaps and silences to undermine its totalizing enterprise. As Roland Barthes suggests, for all that language strives to make the body whole, it has as well a certain "spitefulness":

> Spitefulness of language: once reassembled, in order to *say* itself, the total body must return to the dust of words, to the apportioning of details, to the monotonous inventory of parts, to crumbling: language undoes the body, returns it to the fetish.[13]

In just such paradoxical fashion madness and the body's fragments, in Maupassant's "Qui sait?" belong in fact to this tale's textual "reason"; they provide us with its textual "unity" while also provoking a kind of textual explosion into which both reader and protagonist are thrown. It is as though the fragments of madness, like those of the body in pieces, like those of language itself, simultaneously supplied the grammar and exploded the story. Indeed, it seems they produce together their greatest effect. They form a kind of rhetoric of the fragment—a baring of language, a dismembering of the body, a "narration" of madness, that perfectly undoes every possible whole, while also bringing to their mutual project an uncanny semblance of unity. Language contributes to this its totalizing enterprise; madness, its infinite reserve of possible meaning; the body, even in pieces, its ultimate attachment to nature. One thinks of Gilles Deleuze's suggestion that partial objects are essentially "menacing, tumultuous, toxic, venomous," not so much because they are partial but because in fact they are such dangerous "wholes."[14]

From this tension comes what I perceive to be the "naturalness" in a tale such as Maupassant's "Qui sait?"—the sense in which its events fall far more on the side of the familiar than the alien, while the narrator's terror comes down on the side of the reasonable. There is an eerie logic in the exodus of the narrator's furniture, an eerie logic in the explosion that rattles his house. This text unites conflicting categories within the most usual modulations of language—unites the animate with the inanimate, self with other, interiors with exteriors, houses and objects with bodies and body parts, and unites these with "uncanny" ease (indeed, at times, almost without our noticing) when to unify such opposing terms is to so undermine ontological security that in the end, as the narrator will finally lament, "the prisons themselves are not secure" (1237). Bodies have been exchanged with objects, the narrator himself finds a fearful double in the antiquarian he meets, while the tale itself refuses either to close or to distinguish clearly between the story's past and a possible present—between a narrator who recounts the tale as if entirely in retrospect and one who now waits inside the asylum. In the narrator's lingering fear *not* of his furniture but of the antiquarian, "that monster with a lunar cranium" (1236), product, perhaps, of his own self-splitting, he tells us at the story's conclusion:

> And I am alone, alone, completely alone, three months now. I am at peace, mostly. I have only one fear . . . What if the antiquarian went mad . . . and what if they brought him to this asylum . . . The prisons themselves are not secure. (1237)

*

> What fascinates us is always that which radically excludes us, either by its logic or by its internal perfection.
>
> —Jean Baudrillard, "Fétichisme et idéologie: la réduction sémiologique"

It has not been the intent of this chapter to presume to understand the nature of madness, a term that has occupied and often defied the best of critics. Whether considered in its thematic dimension (Tzvetan Todorov) or as an index of the spirit of a time (Tobin Siebers), as historically repressed (Foucault), linguistically mediated (Derrida), or as the distinctive privilege of literature (Shoshana Felman), madness invariably eludes our critical/theoretical grasp. Still, I hope to have shown that to whatever degree we follow its meanings, and with whatever stakes, madness plays a crucial role in fantastic narrative. This form provides for madness the perfect arena, narrates its rebellious parts without containing them, while the hesitation that underlies our own reason's relation to madness makes of madness a privileged partner for the literary fantastic. Fantastic narrative, it seems to me, is built more than anything else upon its rhetoric of the fragment, and to this rhetoric madness is often able to add its own particular language of partial objects.

Just as the fragmented body in fantastic narrative, moreover, is often encountered as female, so madness, though most often the property of male protagonists, takes most readily a feminine shape. It is "embodied," it would seem, as La Belle Morte of "La Chevelure" (the female body "revived" from the mesh of hair), and in the narrator's cousin Berenice in the tale by Poe. In "Qui

sait?" it would seem to reside in that house in which the narrator
feels as happy "as though clasped in the arms of a woman" (1226),
while in "Le Divorce," a tale Maupassant would write in 1888,
the narrator fears those invasive thoughts that enter our mind,
any one of which may turn out to be "a female invader [*une en-
vahisseuse*], a mistress, a tyrant, [that] . . . installs itself, chases
away all our ordinary preoccupations, absorbs all our attention
and changes the optic of our judgment" (*Œuvres complètes*, 2:
1018). In Nerval's *Aurélia*, similarly, as Shoshana Felman points
out, if the author "examines himself and his madness under a
feminized title, it is because 'woman' symbolizes that locus of
lack around which his delirium crystallizes. 'Aurélia' is not, in
reality, a female character in the narrative, but the nominal force
of an absence, a signifier of loss. From the outset, and at the very
sources of the story, she is *named* precisely as what is *lost*."[15]

There is a way in which madness, despite internal division,
creates for itself its own peculiar unity, determines its own convincing "real." And this real, it would seem, is as good as any. As
Jane Gallop writes, "Avoiding delusion . . . is not a possible alternative. There is no direct apprehension of the real, no possible
liberation from imagoes, no unmediated reading of a text."[16] So
too, as I hope to have shown in Chapter 3, the fantastic partial
body hovers between more tangible and more figural significations in order finally to acquire its own particular, redefined, eccentric yet convincing outline. It takes on, in the gaze of the protagonist and within the explosive dynamic of the text, a status
that is a confounding of language, a confounding of the Symbolic, a transformation even of the Imaginary. It becomes a body
of madness—the teeth of Berenice, "le horla" crouched upon a
narrator's chest, the rebellious hand in "Le Tic," the foot of *La
Belle-Noiseuse*, the house in "Qui sait?"—for the way it both represents confusion and overcomes this, for the way it deftly
"names" that confusion (as though this were susceptible of nam-
ing) by the very definitiveness of its physical contours. In the end
this body emerges as a product of wild division, yet outlines a
strikingly persuasive whole, attesting to an easiness with its own

fragmented shape that naturalizes its severed origins. It is this easiness with its own divided nature, indeed, that is so extraordinary,
and so convincing, in that piano "à queue" (grand piano—literally, piano "with a tail") when it gallops away "with a murmur
of music in its flank," or in Berenice's teeth when they become a
"ghastly" spectrum, or in the dresser when it is turned to erotic
body. These parts insist with all the confident power of a "real"
that is comfortably sure of itself, with a real that is—and this
compellingly—its own most "natural" supernatural.

If I have implied throughout this book that fantastic narrative
is most perfectly seen in its "sliding" of meaning—in its multi-
valent, fragmented body, for example—I would add to this that
such terms as "madness" inhabit its texts as further marks of instability, as "reasonable" challenges to interpretive reason, as in-
dications that what is profoundly at stake in each text is in fact its
own internal, interpretive project. Madness may take its logic
from that body of language whose grammar, as Derrida suggests, is constitutively "normal," and the fragmented body its
partial, "unnatural" shape from the very nature we presume to
know. And yet each one, with the tools of reason, formulates the
unreasonable and disrupts meaning, excluding us in the final
analysis to the very degree that we would banish it.

CHAPTER 5

Dickens, Eliot, Balzac, Flaubert, and The Body Reassembled

REALISM'S GREAT EXPECTATIONS

> It is because "real life" is nothing other than a gaping hole
> that Dream, little by little, pours into it. . . . In the hollow
> of the real grows a compensatory delirium . . . [that] end-
> lessly strives to reunite the lovers, to recapture the lost ob-
> ject, to re-establish a cosmic harmony.
>
> —Shoshana Felman, "Gérard de Nerval: Writing Living,
> or Madness as Autobiography"

If nineteenth-century fiction is marked especially by that insistent effort of the realist novel to contain the fragment, to narrate a totalizing *comédie humaine* for the proliferating pieces of a radically partialized, object-filled world, fantastic narrative, striking instead for its promotion of the fragment, would seem by contrast to afford the nineteenth century a domain for uncontrollable excess, for unincorporable detail, and for madness. Here the fragment—the foot emerging from the corner of the canvas in Balzac's "Chef-d'œuvre inconnu," the vulture eye and beating heart in Poe's "Tell-Tale Heart," the seductive mesh of hair in Maupassant's "La Chevelure"—resists totalization, threatens at every moment to explode the narrative in which it occurs, provides an energy that obliges narrative plotting itself to chart its course through a precarious and unstable debris of pieces.

And yet for all its divided psyches, its partial objects, its dis-

Fig. 5.1 Marcus Stone, Mr. Venus Surrounded by the Trophies of His Art, from Charles Dickens, Our Mutual Friend, 1869

membered limbs, its dissimilarity to the structured wholes of the realist novel, fantastic narrative would seem also to be an anguished gesture toward a differently envisioned wholeness, often finding in the isolated piece its own special version of ontological unity. When the narrator of Poe's "Berenice" unburies his cousin and extracts her teeth from her body he betrays a desire, in the face of a world shattering all about him, to make of its pieces the bearers of a separate fullness and a meaningful essence. He renders Berenice's teeth whole, in a sense, in assigning to them "a sensitive and sentient power, and . . . a capability of moral expression" (216). In Maupassant's "La Chevelure," similarly, the mesh of hair with which the madman is enamored becomes for him, in that epiphanic moment toward the end of the tale, a female body that is entirely complete, one that he may now possess (or so he says) as it was when living. To collect parts of things, as I have noted and as Jean Baudrillard points out, is to be interested in whatever is "factitious, differential, coded, systematized" in the object (*Le Système des objets*, 216)—whatever may be abstracted from the object and woven into an invulnerable world where "real" values might be exchanged for a homogeneous system of signs and where, in the last analysis, the partial body might be whole and complete.

Fantastic narrative depends, further, on rhetorical modes and devices characteristic of the realist novel, repeating, if magnifying, the novel's descriptive strategies, bringing to life strikingly similar images, betraying like preoccupation with material detail. In texts by Hoffmann, Poe, Maupassant, Gautier, Mérimée, Hawthorne, and Villiers de l'Isle-Adam, extraordinary effects emerge again and again without the text's relinquishing the realist world, so that, for example, Hoffmann's "Ritter Gluck" (1809) stages its fantastic moments while barely straying from the mundane and bustling square in Berlin with which it opens. It is a square where we find not haunting shadows but instead a "gaudy stream of people" wandering along the Lindenstrasse, occupying tables "at Klaus's and at Weber's" and quarreling "about war and peace, about Mademoiselle Bethmann's shoes, whether they were recently gray or green."[1] When strangers "disappear," as Ritter Gluck does at the end of the tale, they merely vanish "with the light through the door" (24). In Maupassant's "Qui sait?" similarly, before the narrator's furniture tramples its owner in the dust it is anchored solidly within a narration that knows the pleasure of admiring the scenery, of savoring the detail, of making precise the temporal moment, of picturing for the reader the realist's vision of everyday things. The exodus of the narrator's furniture is profoundly surprising, yet it develops in an eerily natural way. The narrator returns from the theater, "[his] head filled with sonorous melodies, [his] eye haunted by lovely visions" (1227), during which time he admires the moon, considers the time, and estimates the distance home: "From here to my place," he calculates, "it is about one kilometer, maybe a little more, say twenty minutes at a slow walk. It was one o'clock in the morning, one o'clock or one-thirty" (1227).

In Maupassant's "La Nuit" (1887), we could hardly find a more vivid rendition of Paris streets, of the pleasure of the *flâneur*, of *chiffonniers* and of gas lamps, of cafés, and of vegetable carts on their way to Les Halles. (How much more sober, in fact, is the Paris of this fantastic tale than the Paris of Balzac's short novel, *La Fille aux yeux d'or* [1835], a realist narrative in which, fantastically, "everything smokes, everything burns, everything glows, everything boils, everything flames, evaporates, goes out, reignites, flashes, crackles, and consumes itself.")[2] Indeed, when the streets of Paris become horrific in Maupassant's tale it is only in the subtlest of ways. After walking for hours the narrator realizes that the gas lamps are no longer lit, yet it is far from morning; that there are too few sounds; that his watch has stopped; that no clocks are striking; that no one, when he rings, answers the bell. Desperate, he will run from house to house unable to elicit response, twenty times over pulling on every bell, "beating with [his] feet, with [his] cane, with [his] hands, doors that remain obstinately closed" (2: 948). He calls out for help only to find that his voice flies off "without an echo, weak, smothered, crushed by the night" (2: 947). The silent, darkened streets meanwhile are only the more dreadful for their familiarity to him. Though on other nights he would "cry out for pleasure" as he wandered their sinuous paths, on this particular night it is agony to walk as though blind, recognizing streets only by counting them (2: 947). An exquisite hymn to the night and to the exuberant life of the city, "La Nuit" becomes nightmarish in the end with little more than an extinction of light, reminding us of the power of Freud's notion that terror often arises most powerfully in contexts we know most well.[3] As Marie-Claire Bancquart has noted, Maupassant causes a city to emerge that "haunts the reader with its precise detail, with an everydayness that is impossible to disavow."[4]

Finally, in Mérimée's "La Vénus d'Ille" (1837) we find the prominent use of scientific discourse, once again a proceeding common to the novel. In this tale of a beautiful though menacing ancient bronze Venus on whose finger a groom-to-be places his wedding ring while playing a game of soccer, an antiquarian and an archeologist debate at length the statue's origins and the meaning of the inscriptions upon her. As these two men of science discuss the etymological implications of the words they decipher, and as they gauge whether their Venus is Phoenician or Greek, the unwise young groom returns for his ring only to find that the statue has closed her hand and that the ring may no longer be retrieved.

Fantastic narrative repeats many of the novel's descriptive strategies, dwells on strikingly similar images evoked with similar care, even undermines, from certain points of view, its own promotion of the fragmentary and the incomplete. Its most realist moments, it is true, are often radically turned on their heads. (The Venus of Ille is not just an archeological find bearing all the necessary scientific accoutrements, but a statue that will claim her due on the groom's wedding night by entering his bed and crushing his body beneath her several tons.) And yet this only shows more clearly the proximity of the alien to the familiar and the everyday in these texts, and the fragility of those ontological limits that would seem otherwise so rigorously set. One could almost say that the vision that will be so horrific for the narrator of Maupassant's "Qui sait?" is already nascent in the "lovely visions" he remembers from the theater—visions that are, he says, "haunting" (1227)—while the awful sound that he finally hears coming "from the interior of his house" is generated from the "sonorous melodies" that so pleasantly, and so undramatically, fill his head as he approaches home.

*

Conversely, for all its obsession with unity, realist narrative cannot help but be a valorization of the fragment. One can hardly read the novels of Balzac, Flaubert, Zola, Dickens, or Eliot without remarking on the obsession with detail, on the catalogs of objects, on the way in which the scenes these novels evoke, as critics have shown, are as full of luxurious and meandering parts as ever they are unified.[5] In its effort to "encompass 'everything' . . . within its descriptive grasp" (Alter, *Partial Magic*, 95), in the pleasure it displays in "being able to *see*, as though for the first time, the clutter of furniture, the cut of clothing" (Levine, *Realistic Imagination*, 21), in what Stephen Heath has called its "endless passage from detail to detail,"[6] the novel forces us to remember not just the wholes it makes possible but also such suggestive "pieces" as Charles's hat in Flaubert's *Madame Bovary*, or in Dickens's *Bleak House* the sweeping skirts of Mrs. Paradiggle that knock down chairs and other light objects as she distributes her "rapacious benevolence."[7] Like that Dickensian keeper of bottles and rags who revels in the very disparateness of the objects he collects, the novel too might happily admit:

> You see, I have so many things here, . . . of so many kinds. . . .
> And I have a liking for rust and must and cobwebs. And all's fish
> that comes to my net. And I can't bear to part with anything I once
> lay hold of (or so my neighbors think, but what do *they* know?) or
> to alter anything, or to have any sweeping, nor scouring, nor clean-
> ing, nor repairing going on about me.[8]

But there isn't just a continual and pervasive play of "pieces" in the novel. There is also a sense that these pieces are not always or so easily brought to order. In George Eliot's *Middlemarch* almost every character reflects perversely the gargantuan task that has already brought his or her world together: Casaubon spends his life looking for the "Key to all Mythologies," trying mentally to reconstruct the world "as it used to be, in spite of ruin and confusing changes."⁹ Ultimately he hopes to condense his voluminous findings to the point of their "[fitting] a little shelf" (47). Trumbull, the gentle auctioneer who feels that "trifles make the sum of human things," wishes he had the universe "under his hammer" so that it might "go at a higher figure for his recommendation" (652–53). Lydgate studies "macerated muscle" and "eyes presented in a dish" (380) with the project of one day demonstrating "the homogenous origin of all the tissues" (495). Farebrother lovingly collects, and hopes to complete, his array of "blue-bottles and moths" (201). Mr. Brooke perpetually shuffles his documents for having learned that such ordering devices as "pigeon-holes" simply "will not do" (42). Ladislaw meditates on the fragments of Rome whose "gigantic broken revelations" (225) "stimulate" his imagination "and [make] him constructive" (244). Dorothea shudders at the "days, and months, and years" it might take to sort her husband's notes—"shattered mummies" of a mosaic already "wrought from . . . ruins" (519). Mrs. Taft gathers society's scandals "in misleading fragments caught between the rows of her knitting" (296) while Mrs. Cadwallader presses these all together in a "pickle of epigrams" (83).

Even the reader is pulled into the ranks of those mimicking the ordering task of the novel. At the head of every chapter in *Middlemarch* we are confronted with epigraphs that often fail to make ready sense. These promising fragments—some in lyric, some in prose, some by the author, others from sources ranging from *Ecclesiasticus* to Oliver Goldsmith—tend to remain obscure until we have painstakingly returned to read them in retrospect of the chapter each one heads. It is as though we were required not simply to "follow" the story before us but to construct as well, and on the side, a separate structure of clues—as though the novel meant to proceed in perfect continuity while we loped behind, gathering at intervals an ever-promising but never quite necessary metacommentary.

All these projects are held together by the now powerful, now self-questioning forces of the novel, whose task, however, is always in jeopardy. As D. A. Miller writes, the project of the nineteenth-century novel may be in fact "to produce a stable, . . . centered world," but "this project is inevitably doomed to failure." Indeed,

> whether the failure is greeted with philosophical resignation (to the fact that meaning can never be pinned down), political relief (that a work's suspect ideological messages don't finally hang together), or erotic celebration (of a desire that erupts when and where it is least wanted), it always gives evidence of a process that, while inherent in "the text," nonetheless remains curiously outside and deconstructive of what this text mundanely "wants to say."[10]

In something of this spirit, perhaps, Eliot's narrator implicitly likens the novel's project to the one of a candle held up to a pier-glass "minutely and multitudinously scratched," and whose light "produces the flattering illusion of a concentric arrangement" (297).[11] In the end only Mr. Brooke is fully undeceived, he himself having gone into science a great deal at one time, as he says, only to have seen that, like the use of pigeonholes for documents, "it would not do. It leads to everything" (39).

The nineteenth-century critic Francis Wey felt his century's use of the detail was both "brilliant" and perilous. "I don't think the love of the detail is without danger," he writes in 1845, "and abuse cannot be far distant from [its] great success" (*Remarques sur la langue française*, 2: 384). But Wey felt that the danger lay in the degree to which the detail failed in its task to complete the whole, the way it threatened too easily to move from the status of "detail" to the one of "fragment." He noted that "as soon as [it] adds nothing to the image, no color to the idea, . . . or is not in harmony with the general polish of the work, the detail becomes vicious" (2: 384). I would suggest instead that the nineteenth-century realist texts he had in mind had nothing so compellingly or so seductively before them as matter to be narrated *as* "vicious" details. The question, then, was not whether the detail added to the image, but to what degree the image made possible the infinite and necessary play of the detail. This was, after all, that " 'century of progress' which ornamented its steam engines with iron arabesques of foliage as elaborate as the . . . cut-glass chandeliers and bead-and-feather portieres of its drawing rooms" (Dorothy van Ghent, *The English Novel*, 128). It was a period, as Fredric Jameson points out in his discussion of Lukács's *Theory of the Novel*, in which the objects represented in fiction "tear through the human surface of the work like so much alien inorganic matter."[12]

Fragments in realist narrative, moreover, like those in fantastic narrative, often find a privileged if more subtle site in the body in pieces. In Balzac's *Le Père Goriot* the furniture of Mme Vauquer's establishment is "old, cracked, rotten, trembling, eaten away, one-armed, one-eyed, invalid, expiring," inhabiting the novel as though a set of bodily parts.[13] In his *La Fille aux yeux d'or* the city of Paris is "an always pregnant queen" filled with "irresistibly furious desires" (263), whose streets "spit out cruel miasmas" and whose houses "bathe their feet in unspeakable filth" (261). In Dickens's *Great Expectations* Pip remarks, inside Jaggers's office, "two dreadful casts . . . of faces peculiarly swollen,"[14] plaster casts that will return again and again in Dickens's novel, now sitting "twitchy about the nose" (188), now "trying to get their eyelids open" (352), now playing "bo-peep with [Pip]" (401) or, simply, "congestively considering" (421). In every instance they summarize in their dismembered form a text that is redolent with humanized objects and with bodies that are fallen to pieces—with skylights "eccentrically patched like . . . broken head[s]," with houses that twist and turn "to peep down at [Pip]," with walls that are "greasy with shoulders," with high-backed chairs kept in place by the nails that form their outline and make them a coffin (188).

Even in the novels of Eliot and Flaubert, whose characters and universe are so much more soberly realistic than those of Dickens and Balzac, the body is strikingly present both as a way of imagining the world and as a space irresistibly prone to dismemberment. In *Madame Bovary*, Emma's pride "unfolds languidly" in the warmth of Rodolphe's compliments, "like someone stretching in a hot bath."[15] The memory of Rodolphe remains locked away in her heart "more solemn . . . than a pharaoh's mummy in an underground vault" (487). Emma's belongings, under scrutiny near the close of the novel by city officials repossessing her home, are "like a cadaver in an autopsy, exposed before the eyes of . . . three men" (560). In *Middlemarch*, similarly, the narrator tells us that we are, all of us, "born in moral stupidity, taking the world as an udder to feed our supreme selves" (243); that Middlemarch "counted on swallowing Lydgate and assimilating him very comfortably" (183); that prejudices, "like odorous bodies, have a double existence both solid and subtle" (473). Bulstrode and his group look on mankind "as a doomed carcase [meant] to nourish them for heaven" (206). The universe itself is a body in parts: "death grapples us, and his fingers are cruel" (461); destiny "stands by sarcastic with our *dramatis personæ* folded in her hand" (122).

Where the body is missing we see its clothes. Charles's character, in Flaubert's novel, is introduced through the detail of his hat, while his conversation, the narrator tells us, is so commonplace that "everyone's ideas trooped through it in their everyday garb" (328). Emma finds Charles's platitude "spelled out on his coat" (383). And Léon, standing behind Emma one evening during a card game and finding his boot resting on the folds of her dress, draws back "as if he had trodden on someone" (381). In *Middlemarch* the passions are "dressed in their small wardrobe of notions, [they] bring their provisions to a common table" (196). Bulstrode clothes "his selfish passions . . . in severe robes" and walks with them "as a devout quire" (758). The agony of Rome at Christmas, for Dorothea, lies in part in its red drapery, "spreading itself everywhere like a disease of the retina" (226), while its masquerade of ages makes her own life appear to her as though "a masque with enigmatical costumes" (225). Clothing in Eliot's novel would seem in fact to precede the body (both our own and the one of the world to which we are attached), but only the more to discover it: the narrator contemplates at one point how "painful" it would be for art to represent such things as vultures descending on Noah's ark in crisis, "those birds being disadvantageously naked about the gullet" (365).

But it is the characters themselves whose bodies are most keenly at stake, and who most submit to partialization. If in *Great Expectations* Wemmick, at the office, is almost synonymous with his "post-office" mouth and Mr. Jaggers with his threatening forefinger,[16] in *Madame Bovary* Emma's body is seen variously, in the eyes of her admirers, as a set of exquisite parts, from her curving neck to her oval fingernails. She is, for Rodolphe, "fine teeth, black eyes, a dainty foot, a figure like a Parisienne's" (410), while Charles will see her in the end reduced to chattering teeth, drawn lips, convulsed limbs, and hands wandering over the sheets "with that hideous and gentle movement of the dying" (587). The horror of her suicidal body recalls the dying flesh of Hippolyte's club-foot, decaying inside the unnatural box Charles invents for it. And it recalls the body of the blind man, a "wretched creature" with "two gaping and bloody orbits in the place of eyelids" (534), whose appearance will haunt Emma even in her final moments. As she lies dying her body begins to resemble his: "The whole of her tongue protruded from her mouth; her eyes, as they rolled, grew paler, like the two globes of a lamp that is going out" (588–89).

Eliot's novel is more metaphorical (and in this perhaps more typical of the realist novel) in its preoccupation with its characters' bodies. But it is no less powerful in its bodily images. To be disappointed or unsuccessful in the life that Middlemarch has to offer is to be mutilated: Lydgate comes to realize that life with Rosamond must be taken up "on a lower stage of expectation, as it is by men who have lost their limbs" (702); Ladislaw's frustration in loving Dorothea will require his making a "fresh start on crutches" (861); Mrs. Bulstrode will need some time, on learning of her husband's disgrace, to "get used to her maimed consciousness, her poor lopped life" (806). Even without such disappoint-

ment, and despite the narrator's assertion that "a human being
. . . is a very wonderful whole" (444), each of the characters in
the novel seems inclined to reconstruct and deconstruct the
other's meaning according to that other's parts. Thus Mary Garth
exclaims when Rosamond asks about Lydgate, "How can one describe a man? I can give you an inventory" (141), while Rosamond
herself will become an expert in considering the parts of her husband as a group of "airy conditions" to be "floated through with
a rapid selection" (711). As for Mr. Casaubon's body, persistently
envisaged in pieces throughout, Celia can't quite manage to see
beyond the "two white moles" on his face "with hairs on them"
(42), while Dorothea finds nothing better to delight in than the
fact that he has the "same deep eye-sockets" as Locke (42). Sir
James is "morally pain[ed]" by Casaubon's want of "muscular
curve" (312). Mrs. Cadwaller describes him as "a death's head
skinned over for the occcasion" (117). Ladislaw shudders at the
thought of Dorothea's "beautiful lips kissing holy skulls and
other emptinesses ecclesiastically enshrined" (399). Even the narrator, who throughout *Middlemarch* joins in the revealing (and
somehow sealing) of each character's destiny through the fortu-
nate or unfortunate choice of parts—impressing the reader with
Mr. Hackbut's "glittering spectacles and erect hair" (213), with
Mr. Horrock's costume that "gave him a thrilling association
with horses" (269), with "the slight protrusion of [Mr Raffle's]
tongue" (572), and with Mrs. Waule's "chinks for eyes" (132)—
even the narrator hardly benefits Casaubon's case when in the
chapter where he is first described we read in the epigraph that
"hard students are commonly troubled with gowts, catarrhs,
rheums, cathexia, . . . bad eyes, . . . vertigo, [and] winds" (66).[17]

In both *Middlemarch* and *Madame Bovary*, finally, the body is
not just interesting for the spectacular ways in which it is taken
apart. In its fragmented form it is also often a site of death, as
though the novel registered here both its Gothic roots—roots it
shares with the fantastic[18]—and its own particular recognition of
the failure of the fragment to totalize. While death at the end of a
novel, like marriage, is normally a mark of closure, dead bodies

are often places of excess, of resistant material surplus best re-moved, if removed at all, through such extreme measures as am-putation. In Flaubert's novel the horror of Emma's expiring body obliterates every previous image of curving neck and delicate skin. Hippolyte's dying foot, mangled and gangrenous inside the monstrous machine Charles builds for it, contrasts starkly with its earlier strength—with "[its] moral qualities of patience and en-ergy" (452). The blind man's hideous face, for Emma, "loom[s] out of the eternal darkness like a horror" (589), while his wretched body, uncured by the medicinal salves of Homais, con-tinues for six months to remind passersby of the pharmacist's fail-ure. Indeed, his body is only contained in the end when Homais finally succeeds at getting him confined to an asylum.[19]

In *Middlemarch*, similarly, as though this text worried just a little at all the blooming parts it brings to life—at Rosamond's curving neck, Garth's animated hands, Ladislaw's hair that "seemed to shake out light" (241)—it takes care to do so only at the expense of bodies expiring. Featherstone torments his family with the "rigid clutch of his dead hand," even mingling "his consciousness with that livid stagnant presence" (358), while the dead hand of Casaubon throttles Dorothea's future.[20] Beside Mr. Brooke is the "effigy of himself," an effigy that parrots his frag-ments of speech as it floats before him in its "buff-coloured waist-coat, eye-glass, and neutral physiognomy" (547). Beside the more vital history of Middlemarch are the contrasting ruins of the history of Rome, ruins "moving in funeral procession" (224). Beside Lydgate's desperate efforts to keep bodies alive are the sus-picions that he is merely "cutting up bodies" (481–82), and his anguish at having a wife whom at one point he calls his little basil plant, "that plant that flourished wonderfully on a murdered man's brains" (893). Casaubon's "death's head" contrasts with the exuberant curls of his cousin, while the body on which this head rests would seem to be as dead as his notes, somebody having "put a drop [of his blood] under a magnifying-glass, and it was all semicolons and parentheses" (96).

Death and dead bodies, like the dynamic of fragmentation

and often in complicity with it, provide space, moreover, in which the novel might control female desire. It is true that men's bodies in this narrative form suffer from the forces of death and fragmentation, but their dismemberment serves most often a less damaging, less universal purpose. Thus Casaubon's "death's head" and "dead hand" distinguish him in a negative way from more vital male characters, but the misogynistic fetishization of Rosamond's body by Lydgate, the bodily punishment of Emma Bovary's rebellion, and the violent death of Balzac's "girl with the golden eyes" (whose bloody imprints of resistance cover the room in which she is murdered) serve to define the boundaries beyond which these female characters may not go. Again, in the end both realist and fantastic narrative would seem to underline fervently that there are no bodies exempt from dismemberment—that there is no privileged access to wholeness. And yet the aggressive silencing of the female body in both these forms— through literal dismemberment in fantastic narrative, metaphorical and social dismemberment in the novel[21]—plays a similarly strategic role. As Naomi Schor has noted, the efforts of the nineteenth-century novel to circumscribe a particular social universe effect a suppression of, simultaneously, female energy and aspiration. In her words, "The binding of female energy is one of (if not) the enabling conditions of the forward movement of the 'classical text.' Realism is that paradoxical moment in Western literature when representation can neither accommodate the Otherness of Woman nor exist without it."[22]

There is a way in which the novel's massive appropriation of teeming objects is always an appropriation of bodies and of body parts.[23] In the energy of its ravenous gaze, in the force of its search to contain it all—and this even beyond its effort to possess a "realm of dead things" by "projecting the qualities of human agents into [it]" (Alter, *Partial Magic*, 96)—the novel can't help but transform its material into a substance that will be homogeneous and whole: into a body, so to speak, ready either to digest new parts or to be digested by the appetite of the form itself. Hence, in *Middlemarch*, the sustenance that living bodies seem to take from bodies expiring, and the homogeneity of a world in which the sum of characters' parts promises a balanced account.[24] Hence, in Balzac's *La Fille aux yeux d'or*, that realm in Paris "where the interests of the city are digested and where . . . the crowd moves about and is agitated by a bitter and envenomed intestinal movement" (256). Hence, in Dickens's *Bleak House*, that infinite round of digestion, assimilation, and exchange that both animates the world and gives it a common heartbeat: the Lord High Chancellor and the Court of Chancery invade and become the body and the warehouse of Krook; Tom-all-Alone's, like a "ruined human wretch," breeds a coiling "crowd of foul existence" (272); Bleak House falls with its owner to pieces for having, just like him, its "brains . . . blown out" (146); while Richard Carstone, like that house, loses his youth and falls apart with that "ruin of youth which is not like age" (878).

It is not surprising that in the consuming world of the novel such radically eccentric characters and environments as those of Dickens and Balzac find their place so easily beside those of Eliot and Flaubert. There is nothing disjunctive between characters " 'thinged' into one of their own bodily members"[25] or of houses "that twist and turn to peep down at [Pip]" and a narrative form that takes every disparate part as a vessel into which it might infuse new life. (Indeed, and for similar reasons, it is not surprising that Dickens and Balzac moved so easily between two genres, as comfortable writing realist novels as fantastic tales.) But the unity the novel achieves when it engulfs and in this way "embodies" the world is always threatened. The novel may certainly be a kind of "warehouse" where, like the one of Krook, "everything seem[s] to be bought, and nothing to be sold" (*Bleak House*, 99), but its infinite round of "digestion" masks the threat of expulsion: the body it envisions requires an endless, sometimes tortuous circulation of parts. Indeed, and with each transaction, some part is often left behind. The lawsuit of the Court of Chancery, in *Bleak House*, may neatly melt away into the mud and mire of Chesney Wold, but the body of Krook, dissolved in a strange event of "Spontaneous Combustion" (512), leaves behind for its baffled onlookers a "charred and broken log of wood" (511), while his warehouse continues to ooze a "stagnant, sickening" substance that "slowly drips, and creeps away down the bricks . . . [and] lies in a little thick nauseous pool" (509). As for Emma Bovary's body, finally at peace and being readied for burial, it is barely raised by the women attending it when "a rush of black liquid pour[s] from her mouth, as if she were vomiting" (594).

I may have suggested that fantastic narrative represents the pieces, the realist novel the ultimate wholes of a world especially characterized by its proliferating parts. And yet, just as fantastic partialization seems simultaneously to reflect a certain desire for the whole, so realist narrative is profoundly obliged to assemble its text, to formulate its particular brand of unity from the most disparate fragments, to construct the human body itself in ways that betray its careful patchwork of pieces. It may be true, as Leo Bersani has noted, that "the realistic novelist can wander, linger, and digress as much as he likes, he will absorb any material . . . into a commanding structure of significance" (*A Future for Astyanax*, 53). Still, the very details that make up the novel's "commanding structures" link it simultaneously and indissolubly to those fragments that surround, and abound within, its own protected domain.

*

A totality that can be simply accepted is no longer given to the forms of art: therefore they must either narrow down and volatilise whatever has to be given form to the point where they can encompass it, or else they must show polemically the impossibility of achieving their necessary object and the inner nullity of their own means. And in this case they carry the fragmentary nature of the world's structure into the world of forms.

    —Georg Lukács, *Theory of the Novel*

The admirable thing about the fantastic is that it is no longer fantastic: there is only the real.

    —André Breton, "Surrealism and Painting"

This body that is torn and ripped apart . . . the artist . . . reassembles it into a total body. . . . And yet, without the

subject's knowing this, . . . this saving body remains a fic-
tive body, . . . an object of which the *underneath*, the empty
interior, will continue to excite his unease, his curiosity, and
his aggression.[26]

—Roland Barthes, *S/Z*

I am not proposing that we collapse into identity the powerful difference between fantastic and realist narrative—the sense in
which the one is continually pressing toward, the other away
from, totalization. And yet it would seem to me their ultimate
projects reflect a richly suggestive complementarity. Fantastic
narrative stages, with crucial difference from the novel, a move
that is endlessly promoting anxiety. It promises only an increase
in fragments, relishes such "perfect" endings as the one of Balzac's "Chef-d'œuvre inconnu" where a painter's careful images
disappear in a flurry of the incomplete. It delights in the way the
narrator of Poe's "Berenice" is left at the end of that tale staring
helplessly at thirty-two "white, and ivory-looking substances"
scattered across the floor, as it does in Maupassant's "Qui sait?"
where the narrator wonders from his asylum whether his safety
is sure when that moon-headed antiquarian might at any time desire to join him. The body that it figures, moreover, is one that it
leaves disjointed: it is *ever* the fragment, and the loss of wholeness
this continually implies, that its texts appear to cherish.

Still, fantastic narrative is compelling for what it shares with
realism: for its preoccupation with material objects; for its attention to physical detail; for its efforts to describe its world in the
terms of the familiar; for its promotion of parts as a cover for an
alternative search for the whole; for its construction of the alien
in the terms of a body that even in its dismembered form (or perhaps especially in its dismembered form) we know quite well.

Realist narrative mirrors this doubleness. On the one hand,
as has often been noted, it begins rather than ends with instability
in order to stage a return to stasis; it is built upon fragments but
in order to coerce, as it were, some larger whole. The novel "baf-
fles us" with its enormous details, as D. A. Miller has noted, yet
"encourages us to anticipate the end of bafflement. . . . [It] dra-

matizes the liabilities of fragmentation and postponement within the hopeful prospect that they will eventually be overcome" (*The Novel and the Police*, 89–90). Thus in *Middlemarch* the various and infinite projects of the characters, as well as the effects of such detrimental parts as Casaubon's and Featherstone's hands, appear to find conclusion in the aesthetic bond provided by the novel's "finale." Here Featherstone's hand is put to rest with the rejuvenating story of Mary Garth and Fred Vincy, while the distressed Brooke family is "made whole again" at the birth of a child to Dorothea and Ladislaw (894). In *Madame Bovary* the moral chaos of Emma's desperate final efforts, the disarray of hidden love letters, the flailing and failed attempts of Charles to interpret Emma's moods and actions, all culminate in almost horrific superclosure as we read not just of Emma's suicide but also of Charles's subsequent despair, ruin, and death, and of Emma's daughter falling to a life of poverty. In *The Mill on the Floss* the conflicting movements and desires of character and of plot are similarly, if more dramatically, rendered null when Maggie and Tom are engulfed by a flood of "huge fragments" (the very objects the text has sought to narrate), fragments that, like them, "[cling] together in fatal fellowship," making "one wide mass across the stream" and passing them by "in hideous triumph."[27] In Balzac's *Le Père Goriot* the fragment almost disappears for the sheer weight of a surrounding descriptive mass so all-inclusive that characters and their environment literally blend together. In Dickens's *Great Expectations* the two dreadful casts, Wemmick's post-office mouth, Molly's cross-hatched wrists, Miss Havisham's rotting wedding cake (that crawls with spiders and beetles, is covered in deadly black fungus, and holds a place for Miss Havisham's body itself) are parts that add up in the end to a convincing sum; they play out, even bring to fruition, the novel's underlying effort at achieving not just a picture that coheres but also a truth that makes that picture significant. The novel's detail emerges, even when useless, as something that would seem in the end "to fit"; it emerges as a "reality effect" (to use the phrase of Roland Barthes) that denotes, in its very uselessness, the literal, material, "real" weight of the world it seeks to represent. As for the body the novel dismembers, it is always at least moving toward reassembly. One thinks of Mr. Venus in Dickens's *Our Mutual Friend*, pictured on this chapter's frontispiece, collecting his "bones warious . . . bottled preparations, warious . . . dogs . . . ducks . . . glass eyes, warious" in his constant effort to construct completed specimens.[28] The parts the novel covets are not more "vicious" than the narrative drive to contain them.

On the other hand, realist narrative can't help but appear in certain lights radically fantastic—as it turns to "real" fragments that, when not in fact demonically charged, one would have thought too resistant to the orderliness into which they are pressed, and as it reveals, in pieces, the very body it so determinedly desires to protect. If the novel's project must always be to reassemble the world (and the body) to wholeness, that body still remains, like the body of Dickens's Richard Carstone at the settlement of his suit, slumped in a corner and stopped from speaking by a "mouth . . . full of blood" (924), a body that resists any neat conclusion. Like the body of Krook that mysteriously self-destructs, leaving behind its charred log of wood, and like Emma's body, still producing horror well after her death, it is susceptible to its own self-engendered "corrupted humours" (*Bleak House*, 512). Indeed, like the bodies both of Eliot's Casaubon and of Dickens's Tulkinghorn, successful in their ambitious efforts to engulf and master the bodies of others, the body the novel would reassemble remains, in the end, a servant to its own unruly parts as it walks in its chambers "noiselessly" up and down, "grasp-[ing] one of [its] veinous wrists with [its] other hand, and holding it behind [its] back."[29]

Perhaps this is why the projects of these two narrative forms ultimately intersect. This study began with a discussion of Balzac's "Chef-d'œuvre inconnu" and the way in which this tale so vividly illustrates the "catless grins" mischievously at play in fantastic narrative. And yet this text, so full of fragments and partial moments, could just as easily be read as a testing of the ideals and possibilities of realism. If in my first chapter I spoke of the fragments that emerge throughout this text as Frenhofer seeks, but finally fails, to "bring to life" his *Belle-Noiseuse*, I would emphasize now that his desire to capture life completely, to defy the very proportions of his canvas through layers upon layers of paint—his conviction that one has only to persevere "until nature at the last stands bare to the gaze" (395)—is surely, on the level of description in language, a dream of mimesis taken to its furthest extreme. If I noted the way in which the masterpiece he seeks is a perfected essence that the text both continually defers but also tantalizingly asks us to believe possible, it was because it was the realist's dream that, along with Frenhofer, we as readers had made our own. (Hence, I would suggest, the surprise we feel in the unveiling of *La Belle-Noiseuse* when the woman it depicts does *not* step gracefully down from her canvas.) If I emphasized the wonderful fragments that seem in this tale to come to life despite Frenhofer's anguished complaint that an image does not "live" until the final stroke has been applied, I would underline now the way wholes and parts are repeatedly and inextricably fused in this text. Hence Frenhofer's insistence that "every face is a world" (395); hence his illustration of perfected completion through the example of the hand of one's mistress. Hence, too, the double viewing of *La Belle-Noiseuse* when it is finally brought from behind its veil—a viewing that includes the disappointed looks of Porbus and Poussin (struck with the inadequacy of Frenhofer's painting), simultaneous with Frenhofer's triumphant pleasure at the perfect wholeness of the portrait *he* sees. For Frenhofer, the realist's dream of completion has been *more* than wonderfully attained when he exclaims, "Where is art? vanished, disappeared! . . . Have I not caught the very color, the very life in the line that seems to define the figure. . . . But she breathed, I think! . . . The flesh throbs. Wait! She is going to rise to her feet" (411).

In the end, I would suggest, the tiny foot of *La Belle-Noiseuse* records not just the fragments of the fantastic but also the drive to excessive wholeness of realism—the sense in which precisely that which is saturated with meaning becomes the greatest mark of hesitation, the sense in which her foot emerges *as* a detail only for the excess of detail that lies beside it. That foot is, certainly, a valorization of the fragment, a symbol of the way in which the masterpiece of the nineteenth century could only ever have been, in the last analysis, the narration of some one perfect piece. But it is also the mark of a usurpation of the fragment—of the obliteration of its unhappy partialness.

One might say that the body and its discourse both most unite *and* most divide fantastic and realist narrative, rendering perfectly for the one that array of beating hearts and severed hands that tantalize and remain detached, while giving to the other a locus by which the world might finally hang together; yet also providing parts that in the first case double quite nicely as wholes, and, in the second, belie that form's artful and always threatened unity. In just this way the body of *La Belle-Noiseuse* in Balzac's tale is both a fragmenting and a unifying force, offering to its spectators a sample of its essential and always indivisible wholeness (a wholeness perhaps only possible for the reason that it is veiled and framed), at the very moment it draws away, denying the artifice that would seek, naively, to represent it.

For both realist and fantastic narrative it is the disorder that propels narration, the fear of this inspiring the novel, its seductive powers providing the pleasure of the fantastic tale. Like the child described by Freud who first throws out and then pulls in a wooden reel tied to a string, exclaiming "Fort!" as the toy disappears and then "Da!" when it returns and testing in this way the limits of his anxiety, the realist novel and the fantastic tale seem to represent the opposing halves of what formulates, in fact, a single gesture. Fantastic narrative is the "throwing out" of the wooden reel, a questioning "How long can I endure the loss I feel when my toy has disappeared beyond my reach?" It relinquishes closure for the distinctly unclosed, unresolved point of suspension achieved before the reel might have been successfully returned. And it expresses this again and again in a body that it relentlessly, even when "lovingly," dismembers. The realist novel, on the other hand, is the pulling back in. At the level of language the meandering parts that compose its detailed scenes are meant to blur imperceptibly into views that cohere. At the level of plot the imbalance necessary to its narration is tolerated for the sake of the nurturing fantasy that comfortable stability will eventually be reattained.[30] It imagines that the fullness of *La Belle-Noiseuse* will not only be reached but will end the story.

Finally, however, just as the child can only manage the throwing out of the wooden reel while imagining that it will in the end return, can only enjoy its return for the pleasure and the fright contained in the throwing out, both forms include, implicitly, the movement described by the other. Fantastic narrative, as I have suggested, often makes of its pieces the coherent wholes it ostensibly banishes, while the conclusive wholes of the realist novel are never as conclusive as they would like to be.[31] As they implicate, complicate, and complement each other, these two forms represent a continuum stretching between, but also uniting, the *fort* and the *da* in Freud's paradigm and along which one could plot other narrative forms of the modern period. They are a paired set of terms in a single imaginative system in which one dreams of, one responds to, the other's movement. Hence the tiny foot of *La Belle-Noiseuse*, functioning in the final pages of Balzac's tale both as seductive, fantastic fragment *and* as the embodiment, in the form of a promise and in the spirit of realism, of a fullness lingering there behind the chaos, a suggested unity that leads Porbus to cry, pointing to the mass of lines, "There is a woman beneath" (412). In its perfectly finished, perfectly failed image, it is a picture of fantastic narrative not just as opposing but as reflective other for the realist novel, and of realist narrative dis-covered in all its fragmented, "fantastic" nature.

Reference Matter

Notes

For complete author names, titles, and publication data for the works cited here in short form, see Works Cited, pp. 151–59.

Introduction

1. Pierre-Georges Castex, *Le Conte fantastique en France de Nodier à Maupassant*, 455.

2. Louis Vax, *La Séduction de l'étrange; étude sur la littérature fantastique*, 310.

3. "The fantastic," they would write, "is the disordering of the imagination or the debauch of genius. . . . It is that assemblage of the most distant genres and of the most disparate forms, without progression, without proportion, without nuance. . . . It is everything that the delirium of a sick person makes him see that is most bizarre" (*Encyclopédie, ou dictionnaire raisonné des sciences, des arts et des métiers*, 6: 682). The *Encyclopédie* of Diderot and d'Alembert was composed of seventeen volumes of text supplemented by eleven volumes of plates and was published between 1751 and 1772. It was an effort to classify systematically all knowledge along Baconian lines.

4. Robert Alter, *Partial Magic*, 114. One thinks as well of George Levine's assertion that the Victorians struggled "to reconstruct a world out of a world deconstructing, like modernist texts, all around them" (*The Realistic Imagination*, 4).

5. Despite Edgar Allan Poe's insistence, in his essay "The Short

Story," that it is the novel, not the tale, that "cannot avail itself of the immense benefit of *totality*," since the novel cannot be read in a single sitting (*The Portable Poe*, 566), there are nevertheless important ways, as I will argue more fully in Chapter 5, in which the novel is able to achieve a more integrated wholeness, even when postponed, than is available to the writer of the tale.

6. In, respectively, Castex, *Le Conte fantastique en France*, 8; Eric Rabkin, *The Fantastic in Literature*, 28–29; and Jean-Paul Sartre, "Aminadab, ou du fantastique considéré comme un langage," 125.

7. In the twentieth century, Tzvetan Todorov notes, "psychoanalysis has replaced . . . the literature of the fantastic. There is no need today to resort to the devil in order to speak of an excessive sexual desire, and none to resort to vampires in order to designate the attraction exerted by corpses." I quote from pages 160–61 of Richard Howard's English translation of Todorov's book, *The Fantastic: A Structural Approach to a Literary Genre*. All future page references to Todorov, in this and other chapters, will be to this widely read translation.

8. Guy de Maupassant, *Chroniques* 2: 257. In 1829 Walter Scott noted, with similar emphasis, that the less naive readers of the nineteenth century were "no longer lured by those [outrageous] fables that had, before, so charmed their ancestors." I take this citation from Castex, who quotes from an article by Scott that appeared in the April 1829 edition of the *Revue de Paris* (*Le Conte fantastique en France*, 6).

9. That there is a relation has not gone unnoticed, but this relation has been seen either as one of opposition (compare my discussion of Todorov below), or as a presence of one form *in* the other, presence that finally serves to keep them apart. The fantastic, it is said, resides occasionally in the realist text as a reminder of other "realities" that might have been narrated; "realism" appears in the fantastic in order temporarily and falsely to reassure (see Jacques Finné, *La Littérature fantastique: essai sur l'organisation surnaturelle*, especially pp. 123–50). More interesting, Irène Bessière speaks of the way in which fantasy is always pointing to, even extending, the "edges" of the real—the way it is in constant confrontation with it (*Le Récit fantastique: la poétique de l'incertain*, 62).

10. For Christine Brooke-Rose his analysis is unsatisfactory for its reliance on the term "ambiguity," a feature this form shares with other genres (*Rhetoric of the Unreal*, 65). Jean Bellemin-Noël, in his "Des Formes fantastiques aux thèmes fantasmatiques," is critical of Todorov's blindness to the important links between the formal (and not just thematic) aspects of the fantastic and the "discourse" of the unconscious.

Tobin Siebers is critical of Todorov for the way his metaphor of hesitation overlooks the relation between violence and superstition, and for his failure to place the structural continuum of the marvelous/fantastic/uncanny in its proper historical context. This continuum, Siebers contends, is "a diachronic rather than synchronic process," in which the "progression from the Pure Marvelous . . . to the Pure Uncanny charts the rhapsodic transformation of supernatural representation in historical time" (*The Romantic Fantastic*, 33). Siebers notes, more precisely, that "folklore and fairytales, in which the supernatural reigns unchecked and unquestioned, represent the attitude of belief found prior to the crisis of Reason. They are pre-Rational forms of representation, although this does not preclude the possibility of re-creating them at any point in time. In fact, the more nostalgic Romantics sought recourse in folklore because it was not contaminated by the Rational skepticism that so displeased them. The Pure Uncanny represents belief apparently overcome by skepticism, where the inexplicable events formerly relegated to the supernatural are placed in limbo to await further investigation" (33).

11. I should emphasize the difficulty of the term "canon" for a narrative form that has most often defied efforts at definition and delimitation. One can say in a general way, however, that it is a tradition that has included especially, in French, selected tales by Charles Nodier, Honoré de Balzac, Théophile Gautier, Prosper Mérimée, Gérard de Nerval, Auguste, Comte de Villiers de l'Isle-Adam, and Guy de Maupassant. In German, Ludwig Tieck is the beginning of the tradition, followed by Heinrich von Kleist and the extraordinarily important and influential E. T. A. Hoffmann, and later by Adelbert von Chamisso, Joseph, Freiherr von Eichendorff, and Hugo von Hofmannsthal. In England, Walter Scott, Edward Bulwer-Lytton, and Joseph Sheridan Le Fanu stand out, while certain works by Charles Dickens, Robert Louis Stevenson, Arthur Conan Doyle, Oscar Wilde, and Rudyard Kipling are occasionally included. In America, Washington Irving, Nathaniel Hawthorne, Ambrose Bierce, Edgar Allan Poe, and Henry James are particularly important, while Fitz-James O'Brien and Francis Marion Crawford are also of note. In the much less appreciated arena of Russian fiction, Aleksandr Pushkin, Nikolai Gogol, Ivan Turgenev, Fyodor Dostoyevsky, Lev Tolstoy, and Anton Chekhov all contribute to the history of this narrative form.

12. Castex usefully observes that the use of the term "fantastic," in describing these texts, originates in Jean-Jacques Ampère's discussion of Hoffmann's tales. Ampère gives to Hoffmann's tales the epithet *fantas-*

tique in the course of a series of articles in *Le Globe* in 1828, despite their title in German of *Fantasiestücke*, or "tales of fantasy" (*Le Conte fantastique*, 7–8).

13. Jacques Lacan's well-known essay "Le Stade du miroir comme formateur de la fonction du Je, telle qu'elle nous est révélée dans l'expérience psychanalytique" (The mirror stage as formative of the function of the I, as this is revealed to us in the psychoanalytic experience) was originally delivered at the Fourteenth International Psychoanalytic Congress, held at Marienbad in August 1936, and with the simpler title "Le Stade du miroir." Its final, revised version was published in the *Revue française de psychanalyse* 13, no. 4 (1949): 449–55. In it Lacan would theorize that in the development of every human psyche there occurs a jubilant moment in which the individual confronts (and recognizes as such) his "specular image" (*Ecrits*, 95). In a "startling spectacle . . . in front of a mirror," the infant gains for the first time, as *Gestalt*, a sense of the "total form" of his body, and conceives the "mental permanence of his I" (94–95). That "permanence," however, Lacan would write, is accompanied by a sense of fundamental alienation; the mirror stage is a moment that launches the individual into a realm that is always mediated by desire for the other. It is a drama that, "for the subject, caught up in the lure of spatial identification, manufactures a series of fantasies, each one succeeding upon the next, first of a fragmented image of the body, then of a form . . . of its totality, and finally of the . . . assumed armour of an alienating identity—armour that will henceforth mark, with its rigid structure, the [subject's] entire mental development" (97). Images / memories / fantasies of a fragmented body—a *corps morcelé*—images that often appear in dreams when analysis "touches on a certain level of aggressive disintegration in the individual" (97) become for Lacan the markers of a retrospectively imagined lack of totality, a lack that was not felt in early infancy but that is generated instead from the very fragility of that wholeness (always an alienated and alienating wholeness) that the self would seem to have acquired.

Chapter 1

1. Honoré de Balzac, *Le Père Goriot*, 22–23. All future page references will be indicated parenthetically within the text.

2. I will return to this tale in a central way in the next chapter.

3. Edgar Allan Poe, "Berenice," *Collected Works of Edgar Allan Poe*, 2: 215–16. All future page references will be indicated parenthetically

within the text. The Belknap Press edition that I cite here adds a diaeresis over the final "e" in "Berenice" (Berenicë) to remind readers that in Poe's day the name was pronounced as four syllables, and rhymed with "very spicy." I have chosen not to include the diaeresis.

4. One is reminded of Jean-Joseph Goux's assertion that painting in the modern era has become "a kind of writing, a game of signs figured according to the mode of linguistic arbitrariness" ("Banking on Painting," 6).

5. Honoré de Balzac, "Le Chef-d'œuvre inconnu," *Œuvres*, 9: 392. All future page references will be indicated parenthetically within the text.

6. Balzac would appear to be more enlightened than his characters on the hazards and injustice of this "bartering." He makes it very clear that Gillette, Poussin's mistress, calculates the strength of Poussin's love by his acquiescing or not to Frenhofer's request to view her.

7. It is unfortunate for Frenhofer that Porbus and Poussin haven't the spirit of the narrator of Kierkegaard's "Diary of a Seducer." Seeing just the foot of a lady as she steps from her carriage, this gallant exclaims: "I have already seen the little foot, and since I am a natural scientist, I have learned from Cuvier how to draw definite conclusions from such details. Therefore, hurry! How this anxiety enhances your beauty!" (*Either/Or*, 310).

8. In a related vein, Kaja Silverman suggests, in her discussion of a film by Werner Fassbinder (*Ali: Fear Eats the Soul*), "it is not so much the body itself . . . which constitutes erotic spectacle," as it is "the representation of the body" ("Fassbinder and Lacan: A Reconsideration of Gaze, Look and Image," 68).

9. For the translation of citations from *Madame Bovary*, both here and in Chapter 5, I have referred to, but also modified, Paul de Man's felicitous rendering of the novel. Page references are to the original French, as always: in this case to the Pléiade edition of *Madame Bovary* in *Œuvres*, 1: 436.

10. It might be noted that Nodier's tale has often been included in this genre's "canon," while Balzac's tale has not. (The very notion of canon is of course problematic here, as I have suggested, since the genre itself has remained insufficiently defined.)

11. Charles Nodier, "Une heure ou la vision," *Contes de Nodier*, 15–17. All future page references will be indicated parenthetically within the text.

12. E. T. A. Hoffmann, *Der Sandmann, Das öde Haus*, 18. All future page references will be indicated parenthetically within the text.

13. Nathaniel Hawthorne, "The Birthmark," *The Portable Hawthorne*, 173. All future page references will be indicated parenthetically within the text.

Chapter 2

1. See Chapter 1, first epigraph, cited from Denis Diderot, *Encyclopédie*, 4: 878.

2. Roland Barthes, "Les Planches de l' 'Encyclopédie,'" 1356. Diderot's *Encyclopédie* was, of course, a massive descriptive project that attempted to record, for the very first time, the full range of human knowledge of the world. It was a project whose didactic nature demanded adherence to a very objective, "real" world.

3. As J.-B. Pontalis points out, just as one can see in totality, whether of person or of body, "a mere support, if not appendage, to the object itself," the part may easily become something chosen *"in the place"* of the whole (*Objets du fétichisme*, 8).

4. In his *Prolegomena* Kant distinguishes between our judgment of experience and our judgment of perception. Descartes points out that "despite the fact that everyone is communally persuaded that the ideas we have in our minds are entirely similar to the objects from which they proceed, I see no reason that might in fact assure us that this is the case; indeed I am aware, instead, of numerous experiments that should make us doubtful" ("Le Monde ou Traité de la lumière," *Œuvres philosophiques*, 1: 315).

5. While I am suggesting that the blurring of bodies with objects is fundamental to fantastic narrative, a consequence and further energizing of the production of parts, this is not to say that the phenomenon is not present in other forms. I will discuss this at greater length in the fifth chapter of this book, in the context of the realist novel—how in Dickens, for example, the body is reified and reduced to gesture and "tic," as Dorothy van Ghent has shown (in *The English Novel: Form and Function*).

6. Edgar Allan Poe, "The Fall of the House of Usher," *Collected Works of Edgar Allan Poe*, 2: 402, 400. All future page references will be indicated parenthetically within the text.

7. In another context I have shown the way in which the observing narrator of "The Fall of the House of Usher" is himself an effect of doubling, an empirical other, another part of this multiple consciousness from the moment he is "ushered" (401) into their presence. See Deb-

orah A. Harter, "Divided Selves, Ironic Counterparts: Intertextual Doubling in Baudelaire's 'L'Héautontimorouménos' and Poe's 'The Haunted Palace,'" 30–31.

8. Théophile Gautier, *Récits fantastiques*, 240.

9. Guy de Maupassant, "La Chevelure," *Contes et Nouvelles*, 2: 109. All future page references will be indicated parenthetically within the text.

10. I take some liberty here in using the term *dresser* since the word that Maupassant's narrator uses is in fact *meuble*. This far more general term (literally, "piece of furniture") presents some awkwardness for a discussion of the tale in English.

11. Fredric Jameson here paraphrases Lukács ("The Case for Georg Lukács," 166).

12. Todorov suggests that the very structure of "hesitation" central to this narrative form is best created and best maintained in shorter texts. My own sense, and this is underlined with the example of Villiers's novel, is that it is only the realist form of the novel (but this is of course the form of the novel we know most thoroughly), with its specifically totalizing project, that, for reasons I will discuss in Chapter 5, lends itself poorly to "fantastic" effects.

13. Villiers de l'Isle-Adam, *L'Eve future*, 45. All future page references will be indicated parenthetically within the text.

14. A colleague of mine, William Sharpe, noted to me how much Edison's description of Evelyn Habal reminded him of V in Thomas Pynchon's *V*, who in the end is nothing more than a bunch of pieces, totally disassembled on the island of Malta.

15. I cite from Pierre Citron's "Introduction" to Villiers's *L'Eve future*, 17.

16. With somewhat different emphasis Marie-Hélène Huet has discussed the way in which the replacement of Hadaly for Alicia is far too perfect. "The very perfection of the imitation," indeed, "undoes the . . . function of representation" and, in this, is "monstrous" ("Living Images: Monstrosity and Representation," 80).

17. Sigmund Freud, "Fetishism" (1927), *SE*, 21: 154.

18. "Metaphor, because few such remarkable examples exist of conceptual migration: just like the sort of objects it would name, the term fetishism always comes from elsewhere!" (J.-B. Pontalis, *Objets du fétichisme*, 12).

It is difficult, of course, to think of the fetish as more than *principally* metaphoric. Like any "signifier," its signification is both some original signified as well as an endless paradigmatic chain of metaphorically interacting signifiers, and a locus on a syntagmatic chain of metonymically interacting signifiers (the text in question).

Chapter 3

1. Jacques Lacan, *Les Quatre concepts fondamentaux de la psychanalyse*, 69. In my translation I have referred often to Alan Sheridan's translation of this work in *The Four Fundamental Concepts of Psycho-Analysis*.

2. Louis Forestier notes, in his annotation of this tale, that in this passage Maupassant "takes refuge in the past for fear of a present already devoured by its ultimate mortality" (*Contes et nouvelles*, 1348–49).

3. D. A. Miller, *The Novel and the Police*, 162. The Victorian "sensation" novel, Miller suggests, goes even further, making of "our reading bodies" veritable "theaters of neurasthenia" (146). Here "our bodies are rocked by the same 'positive personal shocks' as the characters' are said to be," and "these shocks have the same ambivalent character of being both an untroubled pleasure . . . and a less tame and more painful *jouissance*" (163).

4. Translation by Richard Howard (*Les Fleurs du mal*, 30–31).

5. *Collected Works of Edgar Allan Poe*, 3: 793. All future page references will be indicated parenthetically within the text.

6. In his discussion, Baudrillard suggests, further, that the passion to possess an object (or person) often revolves around the "discontinuous," the inability to capture the other as an object of desire in its totality: "The other is transformed into the paradigm of the various erotic parts of his/ her body, with object crystallization in just one of them" (141).

7. This, according to Bersani, is the fundamental question in the novels of Balzac: "Est-il possible de décrire un objet sans vouloir dévorer— s'approprier—l'objet, et sans qu'on soit dévoré soi-même par l'énergie de cette appropriation?" (from his lectures on Balzac's *Le Père Goriot* in a course at the University of California at Berkeley on the nineteenth-century novel, 1987).

8. From the televised interview with Jeffrey Dahmer on *Inside Edition, Weekend* on Feb. 14, 1993.

9. In her psychoanalysis of children, Melanie Klein uncovered a logic specific to the Imaginary space of the child in which part-objects, and the infant's phantasies about the maternal body as the receptacle of these, play a central role. (See, for example, her *Contributions to Psycho-Analysis, 1921–1945*, 305–9.) The concept of partial objects in the early development of object relations was already explicit, however, in Freud's work,

especially in his "On the Transformations of Instinct, as Exemplified in Anal Erotism" (1917), as Jean Laplanche and J.-B. Pontalis point out (see their *Language of Psycho-Analysis*, 301–2). It was explored further by Karl Abraham in his "Short Study of the Development of the Libido, Viewed in the Light of Mental Disorders. Part 2: Origins and Growth of Object-Love" (1924). From Melanie Klein's work, finally, Jacques Lacan draws his concepts of the Imaginary and the Symbolic, discussed below.

10. See Anika Lemaire, *Jacques Lacan*, 177.

11. Anika Lemaire notes in her study of Lacan that his notion of the Imaginary "is an infinitely supple conceptual category. It covers everything in the fantasy which is an image or representation of a lived experience pertaining to the castration complex, before its formalization—forever incomplete, of course—becomes petrified in the symbol of the 'Phallus.'" The Imaginary, Lemaire goes on to say, "concerns the intuitive lived experience of the body (the receptive hollow, the erectile form, for example), of the affects (dependence, welcome, gift, etc.), of activity, of passivity, of the will to power, etc., lived experiences which overlap, accumulate and overflow into infinite successions of sensorial, emotional and conceptual jugglings" (*Jacques Lacan*, trans. David Macey, 60–61).

12. Lacan's Imaginary and Symbolic are richly useful for an understanding of fantastic imaging. I use them, however, only in their broadest sense, hoping they might take on, for my own discussion, a suggestiveness beyond their strictly Lacanian use.

13. The terms "mastery and control," in Jameson's formulation, take on, themselves, a gendered significance.

14. As I have noted before, my use of the terms "metaphor" and "metonomy" is oversimplified, intended merely to be suggestive. It would be interesting to place my use of them here in the context of Lacan's notion of desire as protolinguistic and metonymical, its symptoms the product of metaphor.

15. The citation is from Jacques Lacan's discussion of Melanie Klein's dialectic of phantasied objects and is quoted in Anthony Wilden's commentary on and translation of Lacan, in *Speech and Language in Psychoanalysis*, 153.

16. Hugo von Hofmannsthal, "Das Märchen der 672. Nacht," *Sämtliche Werke*, 28: 15. All future page references will be indicated parenthetically within the text.

17. For the translation of passages into English I have used, with occasional modification, the rendition of this tale by Frank G. Ryder, in *German Literary Fairy Tales*. The page numbers given are those of the German edition cited in note 16.

18. Josette Féral, "Antigone," 7. She remains, indeed, what Luce Irigaray has called, speaking of woman in all Western discourse, that "nothing at all, that all in nothing in which every [self]sameness comes looking for what it needs to re-nourish its resemblance to itself" (*Speculum de l'autre femme*, 282).

19. This has been pointed out, Carol Clover notes, by such directors as Hitchcock and De Palma. Thus Hitchcock's marginal jottings for the shower scene in *Psycho*: "The slashing. An impression of a knife slashing, as if tearing at the very screen, ripping the film." As Clover suggests, "Not just the body of Marion is to be ruptured, but also the body on the other side of the film and screen: our witnessing body" ("Her Body, Himself: Gender in the Slasher Film," 213).

20. Below is the poem as he recites it on p. 111 of "La Chevelure," followed by Galway Kinnell's translation:

> Dictes-moy où, ne en quel pays
> Est Flora, la belle Romaine,
> Archipiada, ne Thaïs,
> Qui fut sa cousine germaine?
> Echo parlant quand bruyt on maine
> Dessus rivière, ou sus estan;
> Qui beauté eut plus que humaine?
> Mais où sont les neiges d'antan?
>
>   . . .
>
> La royne blanche comme un lys
> Qui chantoit à voix de sereine,
> Berthe au grand pied, Bietris, Allys,
> Harembouges qui tint le Mayne,
> Et Jehanne la bonne Lorraine
> Que Anglais bruslèrent à Rouen?
> Où sont-ils, Vierge souveraine?
> Mais où sont les neiges d'antan?
>
>
> Tell me where, in what country
> Is Flora the beautiful Roman
> Archipiada or Thaïs
> Who was first cousin to her once,
> Echo who speaks when there's a sound
> Over pond or river
> Whose beauty was more than human?
> But where are the snows of last winter?

. . .

That queen white as a lily
Who sang with a siren's voice
And big-footed Berte, Beatrice, Alice
Haremburgis who held Maine
And Jeanne the good maid of Lorraine
Whom the English burned at Rouen,
Where are they sovereign Virgin?
But where are the snows of last winter?

(Trans. Galway Kinnell, *The Poems of
François Villon*, 47–49)

Chapter 4

1. In this, Shoshana Felman deftly sums up the argument Foucault makes in his essay "La Folie, l'absence d'œuvre." We read in Foucault's essay (I will return to this later), "What we have is a figure that both retains and suspends meaning, harnesses a void in which is only proposed the possibility of a particular meaning arriving to inhabit it, or yet another . . . and this perhaps to infinity" (580). See Felman's "Madness and Philosophy *or* Literature's Reason," 227.

2. One thinks of the illustration Johann Caspar Lavater provides for madness in his *Règles physiognomiques* (1803). It is entitled "Chiffre de la folie" (Cipher of madness), and beneath it he writes: "Whoever smiles for no reason, with one lip crooked; whoever often remains isolated, with no direction, without any determined goal; whoever salutes, the body stiff, inclining the head only forward, is mad" (*Règles physiognomiques, ou observations sur quelques traits caractéristiques*, 61).

3. René Descartes, *Méditations touchant la première philosophie dans lesquelles l'existence de Dieu et la distinction réelle entre l'âme et le corps de l'homme sont démontrées*, in *Œuvres et lettres*, 268. All future page references will be indicated parenthetically within the text.

4. Descartes's arguments are obsessed with fiction, Judovitz suggests, but the instrumental character of this "in the formulation of a new metaphysical foundation is not pragmatically acknowledged, thus fostering the illusion of an autonomous philosophical position" (5).

5. Edgar Allan Poe, "The Black Cat," *Collected Works of Edgar Allan Poe*, 3: 849.

6. Michel Foucault, "La Folie, l'absence d'œuvre," 599. See Shoshana Felman's "Madness and Philosophy *or* Literature's Reason" for a treat-

ment in greater detail of the difference in philosophical position between
Foucault and Derrida on the subject of madness.

7. Guy de Maupassant, *Contes et nouvelles*, 2: 187. All future page references will be indicated parenthetically within the text.

8. Guy de Maupassant, *Contes et nouvelles*, 2: 1225. All future page references to "Qui Sait?" will be indicated parenthetically within the text.

9. Todorov calls these preceding passages merely "an indirect psychological analysis by the narrator" (*The Fantastic*, 88).

10. Christine Brooke-Rose refers us especially to pages 13–14 of Rosset's discussion (*A Rhetoric of the Unreal*, 4).

11. In *Histoire de la folie à l'âge classique, Surveiller et punir: naissance de la prison*, and *Histoire de la sexualité, I*, Michel Foucault uncovers the ways in which the classical age discovered the body as a target of power.

12. Todorov does conclude that Maupassant's "Qui sait?" partakes of the true fantastic, but only because we cannot with certainty attribute its strangeness to madness. Content to locate our "hesitation" in the most banal of structural events, Todorov suggests that because of the *lack* of a framing narrator whose testimony might bear witness to the presence of madness, "there are no preparations for the fantastic [in this tale] before its abrupt intrusion" (*The Fantastic*, 88). Conversely, such stories as "La Chevelure" cannot, for Todorov, belong to the genre. Here, he says, we "know" that the protagonist is mad, since his delusions are framed within the "truth" of an outside narrator. In this case Todorov misses the complicity of the framing narrator who reads to us the madman's journal. As I suggest in Chapter 3 there is a way in which this narrator's "truth," the moment he shivers at the scintillating touch of the mesh of hair, is as unreliable (as mad) as that of the "mad" author whose journal he reads. I should add that Todorov provides, in my view, a sensitive and useful reading of Nerval's "Aurélia," a text where, as he suggests, the question of madness is situated *between* the selves of the narrator/protagonist (*The Fantastic*, 37–40).

13. "Malice du langage: une fois rassemblé, pour se *dire*, le corps total doit retourner à la poussière des mots, à l'égrenage des détails, à l'inventaire monotone des parties, à l'émiettement: le langage défait le corps, le renvoie au fétiche" (*S/Z*, 120).

14. Gilles Deleuze continues, "They are not partial in the sense of coming from some whole for which they are meaningful: it is in themselves and directly that they are fragments impossible to totalize" ("Schizologie," 14).

15. Shoshana Felman, "Gérard de Nerval: Writing Living, or Madness as Autobiography," 69. Mary Donaldson-Evans goes even further,

at least in the context of Maupassant, when she says that madness in his tales "is defined by its feminine specificity: it is an alien being, *l'Autre*, that invades and ravages its host through a cannibalistic activity" (*A Woman's Revenge*, 75).

16. Jane Gallop continues, "The alternative to lapsing into Poe's delusion is lapsing into another delusion, one not shared with Poe, a delusion which is particular, idiosyncratic" (*Reading Lacan*, 70).

Chapter 5

1. E. T. A. Hoffmann, "Ritter Gluck," *Fantasie- und Nachtstücke*, 14.

2. Honoré de Balzac, *La Duchesse de Langeais; La Fille aux yeux d'or*, 246. All future page references will be indicated parenthetically within the text.

3. See Freud's important essay on "The Uncanny" (*SE*, 17: 219–52).

4. Marie-Claire Bancquart, *Images littéraires du Paris "fin-de-siècle,"* 130. As I discuss in more detail in my essay "Silenced by the City: Maupassant's *Flâneur* and Uneasy Dreams," the narrator of "La Nuit" would like to transform the city into some "natural" haven that might invite without threat, to weave through its seductive but alienating fabric his own comfortable, protective veil, to pair the city's blinking artificial lights with the empowering and more reassuring glow of nature. Instead, as it turns out, the night would just as soon exclude the city, the city is a shock to the night, and the self that is seduced by each one is not more secure in their midst. In the tale's final scene the narrator descends by staircase to place his hand in the normally flowing stream of the Seine only to find that its current no longer bubbles over rocks, but is "cold ... cold ... cold ... almost frozen ... almost dried up ... almost dead" (2: 949). We are left with a hybrid and uncanny vision of a city turned to nightmare, of a subject exiled from it, and of nature itself become unnatural.

5. It is always treacherous to make general statements about literary forms so widely studied as the nineteenth-century realist novel: at every point one appears to be saying either too little or too much. As Donald Fanger has pointed out, "Few literary terms have suggested more and signalled less than 'realism.' Originally a philosophical concept supporting the existence of platonic categories; later a causal neologism invented to characterize Rembrandt's refusal to idealize his subjects; in the mid-nineteenth century the rallying cry of a group of French novelists . . . ; in Soviet Russia a strange and constricting orthodoxy—the word persists, and with it the conviction that, if taken out of the hands of dogmatists and sectarians, it may still best describe a special kind of

representation of a special artistic vision" (*Dostoyevsky and Romantic Realism*, 3).

6. Stephen Heath, *The Nouveau Roman: A Study in the Practice of Writing*, 19. As Naomi Schor points out, "To say that realism . . . is a 'detailism' . . . is to rehearse a topos which runs through all of the critical discourses on realism from Brunetière to Barthes, from Lewes to Lukács" (*Reading in Detail*, 141).

7. Even on the largest scale, *Bleak House* attests to a fundamental fragmentation. As so many have noted, its narration is divided into two separate and distinct pieces: into the omniscient present tense of an anonymous narrator and the first-person past tense of Esther Summerson. J. Hillis Miller suggests that this divided telling underlines the vexed interpretive project that Dickens leaves to the reader: the two narrators report what they separately (and sometimes differently) see, each one hiding "as much as they reveal" (Introduction, *Bleak House*, 13).

8. Charles Dickens, *Bleak House*, 101. All future page references will be indicated parenthetically within the text.

9. George Eliot, *Middlemarch*, 87 and 40. All future page references will be indicated parenthetically within the text.

10. D. A. Miller, *The Novel and the Police*, xi. Miller's thesis is reminiscent of Georg Lukács's well-known assertion: "The novel is the epic of an age in which the extensive totality of life is no longer directly given, . . . yet which still thinks in terms of totality" (*The Theory of the Novel*, 56).

11. I widen here somewhat the intention of the narrator's parable, but it is, I think, justifiable. (Are not parables always open to multiple application?) While the narrator reads the scratches on the pier-glass as events, and the candle as "the egoism of any person now absent," I have read the former in the same way, but the latter as the ordering power of the novel. In either case, there is a vision that wants to "illuminat[e]," and bring to order, scratches "going everywhere impartially" (297).

12. Fredric Jameson, "The Case for Georg Lukács," 168. For an analysis of Wey's place as a critic in the nineteenth century, his distinction between "good" and "bad" details in French realist fiction, and his equation of the use of the detail with decadence in literature, see Naomi Schor, *Reading in Detail*, 42–47.

13. Honoré de Balzac, *Le Père Goriot*, 12. All future page references will be indicated parenthetically within the text.

14. Charles Dickens, *Great Expectations*, 188. All future page references will be indicated parenthetically within the text.

15. For the translation of citations from *Madame Bovary*, both here and

in Chapter 1 (see note 9 to that chapter), I have referred in part to, but also modified, Paul de Man's felicitous rendering of Flaubert's novel, *Madame Bovary*. Page references are, of course, to the original source: in this case to the Pléiade edition of Flaubert's novel, in *Œuvres*.

16. Dorothy van Ghent points this out, and notes that it is as though certain of Dickens's characters had been " 'thinged' into one of their own bodily members or into an article of their clothing or into some inanimate object of which they have made a fetish" (*The English Novel*, 129).

17. Eliot takes her epigraph from an 1826 edition of Robert Burton's *Anatomy of Melancholy*, p. 1, s. 2, a text originally published between 1621 and 1638 whose full title (*Anatomy of melancholy, what it is, with all the kinds, causes, symptomes, prognostics, and several cures of it; in three partitions; with their several sections, members and subsections, philosophically, medicinally, historically opened and cut up*) is itself a study in the body in pieces!

18. For an excellent discussion of the Gothic substructures of the realist novel, see Judith Wilt's *Ghosts of the Gothic: Austen, Eliot, and Lawrence*. She notes that many of the realist writers were "clearly engaged in that 'rehabilitation of the extra-rational' that Robert B. Heilman (in 'Brontë's "New" Gothic') notes was 'the historical office of the Gothic' " (102).

19. Naomi Schor has noted that the precise function of the blind man in Flaubert's novel still remains to be pinpointed. He is a character "whose *symbolic* value has for a long time preoccupied the critics" (*Breaking the Chain*, 21).

20. The recurrence in this novel of images of hands is impressive: death grapples us with its "cruel fingers" (461), destiny holds us "folded in her hand" (122), the hands of Garth and Rosamond have lives of their own, those of Featherstone and Casaubon reach out from the grave. Dorothea locates her displeasure in Sir James in the sight of "his dimpled hands" (52). A poet's discernment, according to Will Ladislaw, is "but a hand playing with finely ordered variety on the chords of emotion" (256).

21. One wonders whether there is a connection between the way in which the part, in the novel, functions most characteristically on the level of metaphor, and the fact that both women's and men's bodies become dismembered sites. In fantastic narrative, by contrast, where the body is dismembered far more tangibly, the shattering of the male body must often be read as occurring only implicitly, and behind the shattering of the female.

22. Naomi Schor, *Breaking the Chain*, xi. Penny Boumelha echoes Schor's thesis when she notes, in a discussion of George Eliot's novel endings, that while Eliot "displays the injustices and abuses that press upon

the lives of her women," she then seems, in such novels as *Middlemarch* and *Mill on the Floss*, "to refuse the logic of the insight offered by her own texts, apparently resolving the conflict between romantic, individualistic rebellion and the power of community morality all too easily in favour of the latter" ("Realism and the Ends of Feminism," 325).

23. In suggestive connection to this, Bachelard has noted that "one cannot ponder a mystery, an enigma, or a chimeric enterprise for long without sexualizing, in a more or less veiled manner, its principle and vicissitudes" ("Libido et connaissance objective," 185–87).

24. Even Farebrother's mother and sister and aunt seem to emerge from and survive their furniture, while the furniture takes *its* life from the remains and the reflections of persons now dead: "all the furniture . . . in the house was old, but with another grade of age—that of Mr Farebrother's father and grandfather. . . . There were engraved portraits . . . ; and there were old pier-glasses to reflect them, . . . and the sofas [resembled] a prolongation of uneasy chairs . . . and there were three ladies . . . who were also old-fashioned, and of a faded . . . respectability" (198).

25. Cf. note 16.

26. Roland Barthes, *S/Z*, 118–19. Barthes refers in the epigraph, of course, to the Pygmalion-like love of Sarrasine for La Zambinella, in Balzac's short tale "Sarrasine." La Zambinella's status, for Sarrasine, "is that of a *creation*," the work of Pygmalion *"come down from its pedestal"* (119). Barthes's title for his brief discussion of this in *S/Z* is, appropriately, "Le corps rassemblé" (The reassembled body), a title I echo in this chapter's name, if with a broader implication. (It is not just the artist, but the novel form itself that would strive to make the body whole.)

27. George Eliot, *The Mill on the Floss*, 655. One wonders here what is more hideous—the fragments themselves or the fact of their triumph?

28. Charles Dickens, *Our Mutual Friend*, 62. In his *Dickens and His Illustrators*, Frederic Kitton notes that Marcus Stone's illustration, *Mr. Venus Surrounded by the Trophies of His Art*, depicts the shop interior of a taxidermist by the name of Willis, whose occupation and dingy shop would inspire Dickens with the character of Mr. Venus (200). The illustration, after being drawn by Stone, was engraved by the Dalziel Brothers and appeared originally in the second monthly number of *Our Mutual Friend*, June 1864. The original drawings for the novel are apparently tipped into a copy of *Our Mutual Friend* now at the New York Public Library in the Henry W. and Albert A. Berg Collection. The one reproduced here is from the original Chapman and Hall edition (London, 1865), between pages 60 and 61.

I am indebted to Logan Browning at Rice University for the background on this illustration and to Stuart Sherman at the University of Chicago who first drew my attention to it.

29. *Bleak House*, 631. I use the citation for my own purposes here. It is drawn from Dickens's description of Tulkinghorn in his turret-room.

30. Freud's *fort!/da!* paradigm has been used often and variously by critics of narrative. Of particular relevance to my use of it here, however, is the one of D. A. Miller, who locates, already within the parameters of the realist novel itself, the tension that I find both within but especially between the two narrative forms. In his critical analysis of the ways in which the traditional novel must avoid stability and closure yet simultaneously work toward them, Miller notes that the novel finds itself inextricably caught between the "logic of insufficiency [and] disequilibrium" that constitutes its very "condition of possibility" and the desire for a wholeness that is always greater than the one "such a logic can intrinsically provide" (*Narrative and Its Discontents*, 265).

31. Conclusions are a novel's "weak point," as George Eliot once said in a letter, with "some of the fault [lying] in the very nature of a conclusion, which is at best a negation" (*The George Eliot Letters*, 2: 324).

Works Cited

Abraham, Karl. "Short Study of the Development of the Libido, Viewed in the Light of Mental Disorders. Part Two: Origins and Growth of Object Love" (1924). In *Selected Papers*. London: Hogarth Press, 1927.

Alberti, Leon Battista. *On Painting*. Trans. John R. Spencer. New Haven: Yale University Press, 1966.

Alter, Robert. *Partial Magic: The Novel as a Self-Conscious Genre*. Berkeley: University of California Press, 1975.

Bachelard, Gaston. "Libido et connaissance objective." In *La Formation de l'esprit scientifique: contribution à une psychanalyse de la connaissance objective*. Paris: J. Vrin, 1965.

———. *La Poétique de l'espace*. Paris: Presses Universitaires de France, 1961.

Baltrušaitis, Jurgis. *Anamorphic Art*. Trans. W. J. Strachan. Cambridge, Eng.: Chadwyck-Healey, 1977.

Balzac, Honoré de. "Le Chef-d'œuvre inconnu." In vol. 9, *La Comédie humaine; Etudes philosophiques* 1, ed. Marcel Bouteron. Paris: Gallimard, Bibliothèque de la Pléiade, 1950.

———. *La Duchesse de Langeais; La Fille aux yeux d'or*. Paris: Gallimard, 1976.

———. *Le Père Goriot*. Ed. Pierre-Georges Castex. Paris: Garnier Frères, 1963.

Bancquart, Marie-Claire. *Images littéraires du Paris "fin-de-siècle," 1880–1900*. Paris: Editions de la Différence, 1979.

Works Cited

Barker, Francis. *The Tremulous Private Body: Essays on Subjection.* New York: Methuen, 1984.

Barthes, Roland. "L'Effet de réel." *Communications* 11 (1968): 84–89.

———. *Le Plaisir du texte.* Paris: Seuil, 1973.

———. "Les Planches de l' 'Encyclopédie.' " In vol. 2, *Œuvres complètes; Nouveaux essais critiques,* ed. Eric Marty. Paris: Seuil, 1994.

———. *S / Z.* Paris: Seuil, 1970.

Baudelaire, Charles. *Œuvres complètes.* Ed. and annotated by Claude Pichois with the collaboration of Jean Ziegler. 2d ed. Paris: Gallimard, Bibliothèque de la Pléiade, 1975.

Baudrillard, Jean. "Fétichisme et idéologie: la réduction sémiologique." In *Objets du fétichisme,* ed. J.-B. Pontalis. Special issue of *Nouvelle Revue de psychanalyse,* no. 2 (Fall 1970): 213–24.

———. *Le Système des objets.* Paris: Gallimard, 1968.

Bellemin-Noël, Jean. "Des formes fantastiques aux thèmes fantasmatiques." *Littérature* 2 (May 1971): 103–28.

Benjamin, Walter. *Reflections: Essays, Aphorisms, Autobiographical Writings.* Trans. Edmund Jephcott. Ed. Peter Demetz. New York: Harcourt Brace Jovanovich, 1978.

Berger, John. *Ways of Seeing.* London: British Broadcasting Corp.; Harmondsworth, Eng.: Penguin, 1972.

Bersani, Leo. *Baudelaire and Freud.* Berkeley: University of California Press, 1977.

———. *A Future for Astyanax: Character and Desire in Literature.* Boston: Little, Brown, 1972.

Bessière, Irène. *Le Récit fantastique; la poétique de l'incertain.* Paris: Larousse, 1974.

Boumelha, Penny. "Realism and the Ends of Feminism." In *Grafts: Feminist Cultural Criticism,* ed. Susan Sheridan. London: Verso, 1988.

Breton, André. "Surrealism and Painting" (1928). In *Theories of Modern Art: A Source Book by Artists and Critics,* ed. Herschel B. Chipp. Berkeley: University of California Press, 1968.

Brooke-Rose, Christine. *A Rhetoric of the Unreal: Studies in Narrative and Structure, Especially of the Fantastic.* Cambridge: Cambridge University Press, 1981.

Buisine, Alain. "The First Eye." Trans. Carla Frecerra. In *Towards a Theory of Description.* Special issue of *Yale French Studies* 61 (1981): 261–75.

Burton, Robert. *The Anatomy of melancholy, what it is, with all the kinds, causes, symptomes, prognostics, and several cures of it; in three partitions; with their several sections, members, and subsections, philosophically, medicinally, historically opened and cut up.* London: T. McLean, 1826.

Carroll, Lewis. *Alice's Adventures in Wonderland.* New York: William Morrow, 1992.

Castex, Pierre-Georges. *Le Conte fantastique en France de Nodier à Maupassant.* Paris: José Corti, 1951.

Cazotte, Jacques. *Le Diable amoureux.* Preceded by a study of the author by Gérard de Nerval. Paris: G. Cres, 1920.

Citron, Pierre. "Introduction." In Villiers de l'Isle-Adam, *L'Eve future.* Lausanne: Editions l'Age d'Homme, 1979.

Clover, Carol J. "Her Body, Himself: Gender in the Slasher Film." *Representations* 20 (1987): 187–228.

Dahmer, Jeffrey. "Jeffrey Dahmer: An Interview." *Inside Edition, Weekend.* CBS, Houston, Feb. 14, 1993.

Deleuze, Gilles. "Schizologie." Preface to *Le Schizophrène et les langues,* by Louis Wolfson. Paris: Gallimard, 1970.

Derrida, Jacques. "Cogito et histoire de la folie." In *L'Ecriture et la différence.* Paris: Seuil, 1967.

Descartes, René. *Méditations touchant la première philosophie dans lesquelles l'existence de Dieu et la distinction réelle entre l'âme et le corps de l'homme sont démontrées.* In *Œuvres et lettres,* ed. André Bridoux. Paris: Gallimard, Bibliothèque de la Pléiade, 1952.

———. "Le Monde ou Traité de la lumière." In vol. 1, *Œuvres philosophiques* (1618–37), ed. Ferdinand Alquié. Paris: Garnier Frères, 1963.

Dickens, Charles. *Bleak House.* Ed. Norman Page with an introduction by J. Hillis Miller. Harmondsworth, Eng.: Penguin, 1971.

———. *Great Expectations.* Ed. Angus Calder. Harmondsworth, Eng.: Penguin, 1965.

———. *Our Mutual Friend.* 2 vols. Illustrations by Marcus Stone. London: Chapman and Hall, 1865.

Diderot, Denis, with Jean Le Rond d'Alembert. *Encyclopédie, ou Dictionnaire raisonné des sciences, des arts et des métiers, par une société de gens de lettres.* 17 vols. Paris: Chez Briasson, David, Le Breton, and Durand, 1751–65.

Donaldson-Evans, Mary. *A Woman's Revenge: The Chronology of Dispossession in Maupassant's Fiction.* Lexington: French Forum, 1986.

Eliot, George [Mary Ann Evans]. *The George Eliot Letters,* vol. 2 (1852–58). Ed. Gordon S. Haight. New Haven: Yale University Press, 1954.

———. *Middlemarch.* Ed. W. J. Harvey. Harmondsworth, Eng.: Penguin, 1965.

———. *The Mill on the Floss.* Ed. A. S. Byatt. Harmondsworth, Eng.: Penguin, 1979.

Fanger, Donald. *Dostoyevsky and Romantic Realism: A Study of Dostoyevsky in Relation to Balzac, Dickens, and Gogol.* Cambridge, Mass.: Harvard University Press, 1965.

Felman, Shoshana. "Gérard de Nerval: Writing Living, or Madness as Autobiography." In *Writing and Madness (Literature / Philosophy / Psychoanalysis)*, trans. Martha Noel Evans and the author with Brian Massumi. Ithaca, N.Y.: Cornell University Press, 1985.

———. "Madness and Philosophy *or* Literature's Reason." In *Graphesis: Perspectives in Literature and Philosophy.* Special issue of *Yale French Studies* 52 (1975): 206–28.

Féral, Josette. "Antigone or 'The Irony of the Tribe.'" Trans. Alice Jardine and Tom Gora. *Diacritics* 8, no. 3 (1978): 2–14.

Finné, Jacques. *La littérature fantastique: essai sur l'organisation surnaturelle.* Brussels: Editions de l'Université de Bruxelles, 1980.

Flaubert, Gustave. *Madame Bovary.* In vol. 1, *Œuvres*, ed. A. Thibaudet and R. Dumesnil. Paris: Gallimard, Bibliothèque de la Pléiade, 1951.

———. *Madame Bovary.* Trans. Paul de Man. New York: W. W. Norton, 1965.

Foucault, Michel. "La Folie, l'absence d'œuvre." Appendix 1 of *Histoire de la folie à l'âge classique*, 2d ed. Paris: Gallimard, 1972.

———. *Histoire de la folie à l'âge classique.* Paris: Plon, 1961.

———. *Histoire de la sexualité.* 3 vols. Paris: Gallimard, 1976.

———. *Surveiller et punir: naissance de la prison.* Paris: Gallimard, 1975.

Freud, Sigmund. *The Standard Edition of the Complete Psychological Works of Sigmund Freud.* 24 vols. Trans. under the general editorship of James Strachey, in collaboration with Anna Freud. London: Hogarth Press and the Institute of Psycho-Analysis, 1953–74. Including:

———. "A Child Is Being Beaten" (17: 175–204).

———. "Delusions and Dreams in Jensen's 'Gradiva'" (9: 1–95).

———. "Fetishism" (21: 147–57).

———. "On the Transformations of Instinct, as Exemplified in Anal Eroticism" (17: 125–33).

———. "The Uncanny" (17: 219–56).

Gallop, Jane. *Reading Lacan.* Ithaca, N.Y.: Cornell University Press, 1985.

Gautier, Théophile. *Récits fantastiques.* Paris: Flammarion, 1981.

Genette, Gérard. "Métonymie chez Proust." In *Figures III.* Paris: Seuil, 1972.

Girard, René. *La Violence et le sacré.* Paris: B. Grasset, 1972.

Goux, Jean-Joseph. "Banking on Painting." Trans. Adam Bresnick. *Qui Parle* 5, no. 1 (Fall/Winter 1991): 1–8.

Gubar, Susan. "'The Blank Page' and the Issues of Female Creativity." In *Writing and Sexual Difference*, ed. Elizabeth Abel. Chicago: Chicago University Press, 1982.

Harter, Deborah A. "Divided Selves, Ironic Counterparts: Intertextual Doubling in Baudelaire's 'L'Héautontimorouménos' and Poe's 'The Haunted Palace.'" *Comparative Literature Studies* 26 (1989): 28–38.

———. "Silenced by the City: Maupassant's *Flâneur* and Uneasy Dreams." In *Narrative Ironies*, ed. Raymond Prior and Gerald Gillespie. Amsterdam: Rodopi, forthcoming.

Hawthorne, Nathaniel. *The Portable Hawthorne*. Ed. Malcolm Cowley. New York: Viking Press, 1948.

Heath, Stephen. "Difference." *Screen* (Fall 1978): 51–112.

———. *The Nouveau Roman: A Study in the Practice of Writing*. Philadelphia: Temple University Press, 1972.

Heilman, Robert B. "Brontë's 'New' Gothic." In *The Victorian Novel: Modern Essays in Criticism*, ed. Ian Watt. New York: Oxford University Press, 1971.

Hoffmann, E. T. A. [Ernst Theodor Amadeus]. *Fantasie- und Nachtstücke (Fantasiestücke in Callots Manier, Nachtstücke, Seltsame Leiden eines Theater-Direktors)*. Ed. Walter Müller-Seidel. Munich: Winkler-Verlag, 1960.

———. *Der Sandmann, Das öde Haus*. Ed. Manfred Wacker. 1969. Reprint, Stuttgart: Philipp Reclam, 1972.

Hofmannsthal, Hugo von. "Das Märchen der 672. Nacht." In vol. 28, *Sämtliche Werke*. Frankfurt am Main: S. Fischer Verlag, 1975.

———. "The Tale of the 672nd Night." Trans. Frank G. Ryder. In *German Literary Fairy Tales*, ed. Frank G. Ryder and Robert M. Browning. New York: Continuum, 1983.

Howard, Richard, trans. *"Les Fleurs du Mal": The Complete Text of "The Flowers of Evil" by Charles Baudelaire*. Boston: David R. Godine, 1982.

Huet, Marie-Hélène. "Living Images: Monstrosity and Representation." *Representations* 4 (1983): 73–87.

Irigaray, Luce. *Speculum de l'autre femme*. Paris: Minuit, 1974.

James, Henry. *A Portrait of a Lady*. Ed. Leon Edel. Boston: Houghton Mifflin, 1963.

Jameson, Fredric. "The Case for Georg Lukács." In *Marxism and Form: Twentieth-Century Dialectical Theories of Literature*. Princeton: Princeton University Press, 1971.

———. "Imaginary and Symbolic in Lacan: Marxism, Psychoanalytic

Works Cited

Criticism, and the Problem of the Subject." In *Literature and Psychoanalysis: The Question of Reading: Otherwise*, ed. Shoshana Felman. Baltimore: Johns Hopkins University Press, 1982.

Judovitz, Dalia. *Subjectivity and Representation in Descartes: The Origins of Modernity*. Cambridge, Eng.: Cambridge University Press, 1988.

Kant, Immanuel. *Prolegomena to any future metaphysics that will be able to present itself as a science*. Trans. and ed. Peter G. Lucas. Manchester: Manchester University Press, 1971.

Kierkegaard, Søren. "Diary of a Seducer." In *Either/Or*, trans. David F. Swenson and Lilian Marvin Swenson. 1: 310 (Apr. 4). Garden City, N.Y.: Doubleday, 1959.

Kitton, Frederic G. *Dickens and His Illustrators. Cruikshank, Seymour, Buss, "Phiz," Cattermole, Leech, Doyle, Stanfield, Maclise, Tenniel, Frank Stone, Landseer, Palmer, Topham, Marcus Stone, and Luke Fildes*. New York: Abner Schram, 1972.

Klein, Melanie. *Contributions to Psycho-Analysis, 1921–1945*. London: Hogarth Press, and the Institute of Psycho-Analysis, 1950.

Kleist, Heinrich von. *Sämtliche Werke und Briefe*. 2 vols. 7th ed. Ed. Helmut Sembdner. Munich: Carl Hanser Verlag, 1970.

Lacan, Jacques. *Les Quatre concepts fondamentaux de la psychanalyse*. (Book 11 of *Le Séminaire de Jacques Lacan*.) Paris: Seuil, 1973. Published in English as *The Four Fundamental Concepts of Psycho-Analysis*, trans. Alan Sheridan, ed. Jacques-Alain Miller. New York: W. W. Norton, 1981.

——. *Speech and Language in Psychoanalysis*. Trans. with notes and commentary by Anthony G. Wilden. Baltimore: Johns Hopkins University Press, 1982.

——. "Le Stade du miroir comme formateur de la fonction du Je, telle qu'elle nous est révélée dans l'expérience psychanalytique." In *Ecrits*. Paris: Seuil, 1966.

Laplanche, Jean. *Life and Death in Psychoanalysis*. Trans. Jeffrey Mehlman. Baltimore: Johns Hopkins University Press, 1976. Published originally as *Vie et mort en psychanalyse* (Paris: Flammarion, 1970).

Laplanche, J., and J.-B. Pontalis. *The Language of Psycho-Analysis*. Trans. Donald Nicholson-Smith. New York: W. W. Norton, 1973.

Lavater, Johann Caspar. *Règles physiognomiques, ou Observations sur quelques traits caractéristiques*. The Hague and Paris: I. van Cleef and A. A. Renouard, 1803.

Lemaire, Anika. *Jacques Lacan*. Trans. David Macey. London: Routledge and Kegan Paul, 1977. Published originally in French with the same title (Brussels: Charles Denart, 1970).

Lessing, Gotthold Ephraim. *Laokoon, oder, über die Grenzen der Mahlerei und Poesie*. Stuttgart: Metzler, 1984.

Levine, George. *The Realistic Imagination: English Fiction from Frankenstein to Lady Chatterley*. Chicago: University of Chicago Press, 1981.

Lukács, Georg. *The Theory of the Novel: A Historico-Philosophical Essay on the Forms of Great Epic Literature*. Trans. Anna Bostok. Cambridge, Mass.: MIT Press, 1971.

Maupassant, Guy de. *Contes et nouvelles*. 2 vols. Ed. and annotated by Louis Forestier. Paris: Gallimard, Bibliothèque de la Pléiade, 1979.

————. "Le Fantastique." In *Chroniques*, 2. Paris: Union Générale d'Editions, 1980.

Mérimée, Prosper. *Romans et nouvelles*. Ed. and annotated by Henri Martineau. Paris: Gallimard, Bibliothèque de la Pléiade, 1951.

Miller, D. A. *Narrative and Its Discontents: Problems of Closure in the Traditional Novel*. Princeton: Princeton University Press, 1981.

————. *The Novel and the Police*. Berkeley: University of California Press, 1988.

Mulvey, Laura. "Visual Pleasure and Narrative Cinema." *Screen* 16 (1975): 6–18.

Mulvey, Laura, and Colin MacCabe. "Images of Women, Images of Sexuality: Some Films by J. S. Godard." In *Visual and Other Pleasures*, ed. Laura Mulvey. Houndmills, Basingstoke, Hampshire: Macmillan, 1989.

Nerval, Gérard de. *Aurélia; ou, le Rêve et la vie*. In *Œuvres*, ed. and annotated by Albert Béguin and Jean Richer. Paris: Gallimard, Bibliothèque de la Pléiade, 1974.

Newman, Beth. " 'The Situation of the Looker-On': Gender, Narration, and Gaze in *Wuthering Heights*." *PMLA* 105 (Oct. 1990): 1029–41.

Nodier, Charles. *Contes de Nodier*. Ed. Pierre-Georges Castex. Paris: Garnier, 1961.

Ortigues, Edmond. *Le Discours et le symbole*. Paris: Editions Montaigne, 1962.

Pepys, Samuel. *The Diary of Samuel Pepys: A New and Complete Transcription*. Ed. Robert Latham and William Mathews. London: Bell, 1970–83.

Poe, Edgar Allan. *Collected Works of Edgar Allan Poe*. 3 vols. Ed. Thomas Ollive Mabbott. Cambridge, Mass.: Belknap Press of Harvard University Press, 1978.

————. "The Short Story." In *The Portable Poe*. Ed. Philip Van Doren Stern. New York: Penguin, 1973.

Pontalis, J.-B. "Présentation." In *Objets du fétichisme*, ed. J.-B. Pontalis. Special issue of *Nouvelle Revue de psychanalyse*, no. 2 (Fall 1970): 5–15.

Pynchon, Thomas. *V., a Novel*. Philadelphia: J. B. Lippincott, 1961.

Rabkin, Eric S. *The Fantastic in Literature*. Princeton: Princeton University Press, 1976.

Rogers, Fred [Mr. Rogers]. "Everything Grows Together, Because You're All One Piece." *Mr. Rogers' Neighborhood*. KQED, San Francisco, June 30, 1987.

Rosset, Clément. *Le Réel—traité de l'idiotie*. Paris: Editions de Minuit, 1977.

Ruegg, Maria. "Metaphor and Metonymy: The Logic of Structuralist Rhetoric." *Glyph* 6 (1979): 141–57.

Sartre, Jean-Paul. "*Aminadab*, ou Du fantastique considéré comme un langage." In *Situations*, I. Paris: Gallimard, 1947.

Schor, Naomi. *Breaking the Chain: Women, Theory, and French Realist Fiction*. New York: Columbia University Press, 1985.

———. *Reading in Detail: Aesthetics and the Feminine*. New York and London: Methuen, 1987.

Serres, Michel. "La Belle Noiseuse." In *Genèse*. Paris: Bernard Grasset, 1982.

Shakespeare, William. *Hamlet*. In *The Complete Works of William Shakespeare*, Cambridge Edition Text, ed. William Aldis Wright. Garden City, N.Y.: Doubleday, 1936.

Siebers, Tobin. *The Romantic Fantastic*. Ithaca, N.Y.: Cornell University Press, 1984.

Silverman, Kaja. "Fassbinder and Lacan: A Reconsideration of Gaze, Look and Image." *Camera Obscura: A Journal of Feminism and Film Theory* 19 (Jan. 1989): 55–84.

———. *The Subject of Semiotics*. Oxford: Oxford University Press, 1983.

Sollers, Philippe. "Le Toit: essai de lecture systématique." In *Logiques*. Paris: Seuil, 1968.

Todorov, Tzvetan. *Introduction à la littérature fantastique*. Paris: Seuil, 1970.

———. *The Fantastic: A Structural Approach to a Literary Genre*. Trans. Richard Howard. Ithaca, N.Y.: Cornell University Press, 1975.

Van Ghent, Dorothy. *The English Novel: Form and Function*. New York: Holt, Rinehart and Winston, 1966.

Vax, Louis. *La Séduction de l'étrange; étude sur la littérature fantastique*. Paris: Presses Universitaires de France, 1965.

Vickers, Nancy J. "Diana Described: Scattered Woman and Scattered Rhyme." In *Writing and Sexual Difference*, ed. Elizabeth Abel. Chicago: Chicago University Press, 1982.

Villiers de l'Isle-Adam, Auguste, comte de. *L'Eve future*. Introduction by Pierre Citron. Lausanne: Editions l'Age d'Homme, 1979.

Villon, François. "Ballade des dames du temps jadis." In *Le Testament Villon*, ed. Jean Rychner and Albert Henry. Geneva: Librairie Droz, 1974.

———. *The Poems of François Villon*. Trans. Galway Kinnell. Boston: Houghton Mifflin, 1977.

Wey, Francis M. *Remarques sur la langue française au dix-neuvième siècle, sur le style et la composition littéraire*. 2 vols. Paris: Firmin Didot, 1845.

Wilt, Judith. *Ghosts of the Gothic: Austen, Eliot, and Lawrence*. Princeton: Princeton University Press, 1980.

Index

In this index an "f" after a number indicates a separate reference on the next page, and an "ff" indicates separate references on the next two pages. A continuous discussion over two or more pages is indicated by a span of page numbers, e.g., "57–59." *Passim* is used for a cluster of references in close but not consecutive sequence.

Abraham, Karl, 68, 141n9
Alberti, Leon Battista, 11, 15
Alter, Robert, 113, 121, 133n4
Ampère, Jean-Jacques, 135–36n12
Anamorphism, 12
"Arria Marcella, souvenir de Pompéi" (Gautier), 3, 7, 38–39, 77, 79
Aurélia (Nerval), 106, 144n12

Bachelard, Gaston, 40, 148n23
Baltrušaitis, Jurgis, 34
Balzac, Honoré de, 113, 122, 135n11
—"Le Chef-d'œuvre inconnu," 7–8, 48, 77, 90, 106; and representation, 7, 15, 17–22, 24; and the fragmentary, 15–22, 24, 108, 124; and fantastic narrative, 15, 18, 24, 126–29; quest for wholeness

in, 18f, 127–29; the gaze in, 53–54, 59f; and realism, 126–29
—Other works: *La Fille aux yeux d'or*, 111, 116, 121f; *Le Père Goriot*, 14, 116, 125; "Sarrasine," 148n26
Bancquart, Marie-Claire, 112
Barker, Francis, 88–89, 99–100, 102
Barthes, Roland, 11, 20–21, 28, 58, 103, 124f
Baudelaire, Charles: "La Chevelure," 61–64, 66; "Un Hémisphère dans une chevelure," 64
Baudrillard, Jean, 28f, 41, 47f, 50, 66, 105, 110
Bellemin-Noël, Jean, 134n10
Benjamin, Walter, 28
"Berenice" (Poe), 25, 69, 110; the

Index

Library of Congress
Cataloging-in-Publication Data

Harter, Deborah A., 1950–
Bodies in pieces : fantastic narrative and the poetics
of the fragment / Deborah A. Harter.
p.   cm.
Includes bibliographical references and index.
ISBN 0-8047-2507-1 (alk. paper)
1. Fantastic fiction—History and criticism.
2. Body, Human, in literature.   I. Title.
PN3435.H37   1996
809.3'8766—dc20   95-19134 CIP

Original printing 1996

Last figure below indicates year of this printing

05 04 03 02 01 00 99 98 97 96